# Writing that works

# Writing that works

How to write memos, letters, reports,
speeches, resumes, plans and
other papers that say what you mean —
and get things done

by
Kenneth Roman and Joel Raphaelson

*1817*

**HARPER & ROW, PUBLISHERS, New York**
Cambridge, Hagerstown, Philadelphia, San Francisco,
London, Mexico City, São Paulo, Sydney

Grateful acknowledgment is made for permission to reprint the memo from *Closing the Ring* by Winston Churchill. Copyright 1951 by Houghton Mifflin Company. Reprinted by permission of the publisher, Houghton Mifflin Company.

WRITING THAT WORKS. Copyright © 1981 by Kenneth Roman and Joel Raphaelson. All rights reserved. Printed in the United States of America. No part of this book may be used or reproduced in any manner whatsoever without written permission except in the case of brief quotations embodied in critical articles and reviews. For information address Harper & Row, Publishers, Inc., 10 East 53rd Street, New York, N.Y. 10022. Published simultaneously in Canada by Fitzhenry & Whiteside Limited, Toronto.

Designed by Alan Sprules and Ann Brown

Library of Congress Cataloging in Publication Data

Roman, Kenneth.
    Writing that works.

    1. English language—Business English.   2. Letter writing.   3. Report writing.   I. Raphaelson, Joel.
II. Title.
PE1115.R58 1981     808′.066651021     80-8695
ISBN 0-06-014843-8                  AACR2

85 10 9 8 7 6

*To David Ogilvy,
who has taught us
a thing or two
about good writing*

# Contents

# Foreword

---

## A practical handbook for busy people

This book is for those millions of nonprofessional writers who must use the written word to communicate and to get results—in business, in government, in education, in the arts.

Nothing in it is academic or theoretical. You will find little about grammar, even though good grammar is essential to good writing.

You will find advice you can *act* on, whenever you have to convert blank paper into a letter, a memorandum, a report, a recommendation, a speech, a resume. You'll get help from specific side-by-side examples of good writing versus bad writing.

You don't need a special gift for writing to develop the ability to write effectively. The process of writing is hard work, even for the best writers. But the *principles* of good writing are simple, easy to understand and easy to put into use.

The purpose of this book is to help you say what you want to say, with less difficulty and more confidence—and to get the results you want from everything you write.

---

# Writing
# that works

# Chapter 1

---

# People who write well do well

---

In 1979, *Fortune* magazine talked to many successful corporate executives about what business schools should teach. Interviewers asked:

> What kind of academic program best prepares business school students to succeed in their careers?

Pretty much skipping the question, executive after executive said, in frustration:

> *Teach them to write better.*

This "simple wish," as *Fortune* calls it, was anything but a call for fancy writing. It was a plea to teach a fundamental skill that few people develop these days: *the skill to write with clarity, precision, brevity and the force of logic.*

When you write a letter or a report or a plan, you want something to happen. You may want your reader to:

- Understand your report and endorse your conclusions.

- Approve your plan—and pay for it.

- Send money for your charity, your candidate, your product, your service.

- Invite you for a job interview.

- Know exactly what to do next—and when to do it.

You are not likely to achieve the results you seek if your writing is murky, long-winded, bogged down by imprecisions or jargon, and topsy-turvy in its order of thought.

*Your reader does not have much time.* If you want to hold the attention of busy people, your writing must cut through to the heart of the matter. It must require a minimum of time and effort on the reader's part.

The importance of this increases with the importance of your reader. At any level, readers are likely to be swamped with paperwork. A junior executive may feel obliged to plow through everything that comes across his desk. The president doesn't—and damned well won't.

A senior executive says this about one of her clients:

> *"His desk is usually absolutely clean, but I know that somewhere in that man's life there's a tremendous pile of paper. If I want him to read a memo himself, I'd better get right to the point and I'd better be clear, or he'll just pass it along to somebody else, with a testy little note asking for a translation."*

The better you write, the less time your boss must spend rewriting your stuff. If you are ambitious, it won't hurt to make life easier for people above you. Bad writing slows things down by confusing them. Good writing speeds things up.

People act on matters that have been put forward clearly and coherently. Write well and you'll get more done.

The only way some people know you is through your writing. It can be your most frequent point of contact, or your *only* one, with people important to your career—major customers, senior clients, your own top management.

To those women and men, *your writing is you.* It reveals how your mind works. Is it forceful or fatuous, deft or clumsy, crisp or soggy? When your reader doesn't know you, he judges you from the evidence in your writing.

It is best to stick to standard English usage. We advise this not out of academic fussiness but from observing how things are. If you write "infer" when you mean "imply," not more than one reader in ten will detect your lapse. But that one reader may be the one who counts.

For better or for worse, there still seems to be some correlation between literacy and seniority.

Observant people will note your taste in language as sharply as they take measure of your taste in clothes or your manners. They cannot help forming an impression of you from what they see of you. A large part of what they see may be what you put on paper.

Important issues are usually examined in writing, either in a formal paper or a presentation. It isn't enough that you know all about your subject. You must make yourself clear to somebody who has only a fraction of your expertise. You must express your point of view persuasively. Even a strong position can fail to survive a flabby presentation.

If you expect to get done what you want to get done, and to arrive at your goal—today, this month, or during the decades of your career—you must develop the skill to express your ideas effectively in writing.

Good writing is no guarantee of success. Some people who write well fail. If you write poorly, you may succeed. But Jimmy the Greek wouldn't give you odds on it.

# Chapter 2

# Don't mumble – and other principles of effective writing

M ost people "write badly because they cannot think clearly," observed H. L. Mencken. The reason they cannot think clearly, he went on, is that "they lack the brains."

It follows that if you *can* think clearly, you have a fighting chance of being able to write well. But clear thinking is only the first step. The suggestions in this chapter go on from there. They will help you to put on paper exactly what you have in mind.

## 1. Don't mumble.

Once you've decided what you want to say, come right out and say it. Mumblers command less attention than people who speak out.

Keep in mind E. B. White's sobering injunction: *"When you say something, make sure you have said it. The chances of your having said it are only fair."*

| **Instead of this . . .** | **This** |
|---|---|
| It is generally desirable to communicate your thoughts in a forthright manner. Toning your point down and tiptoeing around it may, in many circumstances, tempt the reader to tune out and allow his mind to wander. | Don't mumble. |

## 2. Make the organization of your writing clear.

When you write anything longer than a few paragraphs, start by telling the reader where you are going. Like:

> This paper proposes that the company invest $1,000,000 in a library.

First you must know where you are going yourself. Make an outline of your major points, in logical order. Place supporting details in their proper position.

Use your outline to tell your reader what you are going to cover—your four or five major points. Underline and number each important section heading. This serves the same purpose as chapter titles in a book.

End with a summary. And keep in mind that a *summary* is not a *conclusion.* Your summary should introduce no new ideas; it should summarize, as briefly as possible, the most important points you have made.

If your paper comes to a conclusion, your summary should summarize that, too. The purpose of a summary is to fix the essentials of your message in your reader's mind.

5

*Summary:* Make an outline; use your outline to help your reader; number and underline section headings; summarize.

## 3. Use short paragraphs, short sentences—and short words.

Six articles start at the top of the front page of every issue of the *Wall Street Journal*. The first paragraphs of these articles are never more than three sentences long. More than half the paragraphs contain only a single sentence.

The first sentences themselves are crisp and compact:

> The U.S. and Russia are glaring at each other again.

> If you think inflation clipped you to the tune of 13 percent last year, think again.

> Among the worlds that Adolf Hitler wanted to conquer was the yachting world.

By contrast, here is an example of the kind of mumbling first sentence that confronts people in their office reading:

> This provides the Argus, Mitchell & Dohn perspective on a consumers'-eye view of the current position and growth potential of Blake's Tea and Jones's Tea, the major entries of National Beverages in the English tea market.

The *Wall Street Journal* now sells more copies than any other daily in America. Readers and editors alike give much of the credit to its readability.

*Journal* editors have put into practice this simple principle: short sentences and short paragraphs are easier to read than long ones. And easier to understand.

As for short *words,* don't turn your back on the richness and subtlety of the English language. Nobody will excoriate you

6

for using a long word whose precise meaning no shorter word could duplicate.

But you should always prefer the short word to the long one that means the same thing:

| Use this | Not this |
|---|---|
| Now | Currently |
| Start | Initiate |
| Show | Indicate |
| Finish | Finalize |
| Speed up, move along | Expedite |
| Use | Utilize |
| Place | Position |
| Cut out | Eliminate |

**4. Make your writing vigorous, direct—and personal.**

People respond best when they are *treated* like people. The easiest way to add conviction to your writing is to write as you would talk. Don't hide behind impersonal language. Use active verbs. Avoid the passive voice.

| Passive, impersonal | Active, personal |
|---|---|
| It is recommended | We recommend |
| He should be told | Please tell him |
| Personal sacrifices are being made, although the degree of participation is not absolutely identifiable. | People are making sacrifices, but we don't know for sure how many or how big. |

Many people mumble along in the passive voice because high school English teachers told them not to start sentences with "I." If that worries you, you can still find good ways to substitute active for passive verbs.

7

Here is a typical passive construction—followed by examples of active alternatives.

*It is respectfully requested that you send a representative to our conference.*

> All of us here hope that you'll send a representative.
>
> Won't you please send a representative . . .
>
> Somebody representing your company would add a lot . . .
>
> Will you give serious thought to sending a representative?
>
> You can see how much a representative from your company would contribute . . .
>
> Without a representative from your company, our conference would be a fizzle.

You might protest that these alternatives don't all say quite the same thing. Exactly! Getting rid of the passive voice not only adds energy to your writing, it tends to push you to decide *what* you want to say.

Try reading what you've written aloud. If it sounds passive and impersonal, rewrite it.

**5. Avoid vague modifiers.**

A businessman writes that a certain outcome "was reasonably unexpected." Just how unexpected is that? Or does he mean that a reasonable person would not have expected it at all?

Depending on what he intended to say, he should have written:

> Few of us expected this outcome.
>
> Although I didn't expect this outcome, it wasn't a complete surprise.

8

State your meaning precisely:

| **Vague** | **Precise** |
|---|---|
| Very overspent | Overspent by $10,000 |
| Slightly behind schedule | One day late |

Don't listen to anybody who tells you to weed out adjectives and adverbs as a matter of principle. They are parts of speech, often indispensable to precise expression. Distinguish between *lazy* adjectives and adverbs and *vigorous* ones. The lazy ones are so overused in some contexts that they have become clichés:

| | |
|---|---|
| *Very* good | *Great* success |
| *Awfully* nice | *Richly* deserved |
| *Basically* accurate | *Vitally* important |

Vigorous adjectives and adverbs sharpen the definition of what you're talking about:

| | |
|---|---|
| Instantly accepted | Tiny raise |
| Rudely turned down | Moist handshake |
| Short meeting | Tiresome speech |
| Crisp presentation | Black coffee |
| Baffling instructions | Lucid recommendation |

Select adjectives and adverbs that make your meaning more precise. Do not use them as mere exclamation points.

**6. Use specific, concrete language.**

Avoid technical jargon. There is always a simple, down-to-earth word which says the same thing as the show-off fad word or the vague abstraction:

| Jargon | Down-to-earth English |
|---|---|
| Implement | Carry out |
| Viable | Practical, workable |
| Interface | Discuss, meet, work with |
| Optimum | Best, largest possible |
| To impact | To affect, to do to |
| Resultful | Effective, achieve results |
| Meaningful | Real, actual, tangible |
| Judgmentally | I think |
| Input | Facts, information, data |
| Output | Results |
| Net net | Conclusion |
| Sub-optimal | Less than ideal |
| Proactive | Active |
| Bottom line | Final result |

NOTE: Popular usage has confused *parameters* with *perimeter*. If you mean limits, say *limits*.

What's wrong with jargon becomes obvious when words like these come at you in clusters, which is how they tend to arrive.

| Jargon | Down-to-earth English |
|---|---|
| It is believed that with the parameters that have been imposed by your management, a viable program may be hard to evolve. Net net: If our program is to impact the consumer to the optimum, meaningful interface with your management may be necessitated. | We believe that the limits your management set may rule out an effective program. If we expect to reach our goal, we'd better ask your management to listen to our case. |

The kind of writing on the left is long-winded and heavy-handed. It is what E. B. White calls "the language of mutila-

10

tion"—it mutilates your meaning. The language on the right is clear and direct. It illuminates your meaning.

## 7. Choose the right word.

Know the precise meaning of every word you use. Here are some words that many people confuse:

To **affect** something is to have an influence on it: *The new program affects only the clerical staff.*

**Effect** can mean a result (noun) or to bring about (verb): *The effect of the new program on the morale of the drivers will be zero; it effects no change outside the clerical staff.*

**It's** is the contraction of "it is." *It's vital that profits keep growing.*

**Its** is the possessive form of "it." No apostrophe. *Its profits grow year after year.*

**Principal** is the first in rank or importance: *Our principal problem is lack of cash flow.*

**Principle** is a guiding rule: *Our principle is to use our own money rather than to borrow.*

**Imply** means to suggest indirectly: *Her report implies that she will soon promote her assistant.*

**Infer** means to draw meaning out of something: *The assistant infers from her report that he will soon be promoted.*

**i.e.** (*id est*) means "that is": *He preferred short names; i.e., nothing longer than four letters.*

**e.g.** (*exempli gratia*) means "for example": *He gave all his products short names; e.g., Hit, Miss, Duck, Dive.*

**Mitigate** means to lessen in force or intensity: *She mitigated the bad news by giving everybody the afternoon off.*

**Militate** means to have force as evidence. Usually used with *against: The bad news militates against an early end to the raise freeze.*

11

**Gratuitous** means unasked for, excessive: *He had done his job to perfection for years. The advice from the newcomer was gratuitous.*

**Grateful, gratitude.** You know what these words mean. The point here is that they have no connection with *gratuitous.*

**Appraise** means to measure, to assess the value or nature of something: *The general appraised the enemy's strength before ordering the attack.*

**Apprise** means to inform in detail: *The chief of staff apprised the colonels of the general's appraisal of the situation.*

**Fortuitous** means happening by chance, accidental. *Being seated next to his ex-wife was fortuitous—and unfortunate.*

**Fortunate** means favored by good fortune—lucky.

**Alternate** (verb) means to go back and forth from one to another: *The coach alternated between passing plays and running plays.* As noun or adjective, it carries the same sense: *Mike and Jim are the coach's alternates; they play on alternate sets of downs.*

**Alternative** refers to a choice among two or more possibilities: *The coach faced the alternatives— go for the first down and victory, or punt to preserve the tie.*

**Definite** is most often used to mean positive, absolutely certain: *It is now definite that the factory will open on schedule.*

**Definitive** means complete and authoritative, determining once and for all: *It was the definitive design for a steel mill, a model for all others.*

12

*Indifferent* means that you don't care how it comes out: *The chairman, recognizing the triviality of the proposal, was indifferent.*

*Disinterested* means neutral and objective: *Amid the passions raging on both sides, only the chairman, recognizing the importance of the decision, managed to remain disinterested.*

*Fulsome* means excessive to the point of insincerity: *His fulsome praise was a transparent attempt at flattery.*

*Full, abundant* are in no way synonymous with fulsome. They carry their own familiar meanings.

*Notable* means worthy of note: *His research on Jack the Ripper is notable for its thoroughness.*

*Notorious* means famous in an unsavory way: *Jack the Ripper was perhaps the most notorious criminal of the 19th century.*

*Into* must be handled with caution. The headline writer wrote, MURDER SUSPECTS TURN THEMSELVES INTO POLICE —stunning as magic, but not what he meant. When the preposition "in" belongs to the verb—"to turn oneself in"—you can't use *into.*

*In to* is not synonymous with *into.* You go *into* the house, or you go *in to find* *your wallet.* You look *into* *the subject* before you *hand* *your paper in to your boss.* The rules are too complicated to help. Be alert to the difference and use your ear.

When you confuse words like these, your reader may conclude that you don't know any better. Illiteracy does not breed respect.

## 8. Make it perfect.

No typos, no misspellings, no errors in numbers or dates. If your writing is slipshod in any of these ways, however minor they may seem to you, your reader may reasonably question how much care and thought you have put into it.

Spelling is a special problem. Good spellers are an intolerant lot, and your reader could be among them. Whenever you are in doubt about how a word is spelled, look it up in the dictionary.

If you are an incurably bad speller, make sure your drafts get checked by someone who isn't thus handicapped.

## 9. Come to the point.

Churchill could have mumbled that "the situation in regard to France is very serious." What he did say was, "The news from France is bad."

Take the time to boil down what you want to say, and express it confidently in simple, declarative sentences.

> *Remember the man who apologized for writing such a long letter, explaining that he didn't have time to write a short one.*

There are only 266 words in the Gettysburg Address. The shortest sentence in the New Testament may be the most moving: "Jesus wept."

Don't be terse to extremes, leaving out words that your reader must mentally replace. Incomplete sentences should be short enough so that your reader can take them in at a glance. *Like this.*

But not like this: *A long incomplete sentence, with a multi-word subject, that sounds until the very end as though it might be a complete sentence.* Such a sentence pulls your reader up short at the end, making him go back to see if he missed anything. (He did. The verb.)

## 10. Write simply and naturally—the way you talk.

Most Americans are taught that the written language and the spoken language are entirely different. They learn to write in a stiff style and to steer clear of personal flavor.

| **Stiff** | **Natural** |
|---|---|
| The reasons are fourfold | There are four reasons |
| Importantly | The important point is |
| Visitation | Visit |

Notice how often somebody will say, "It sounds just like her" in praise of some particularly effective writing. What you write should sound just like you talking *when you're at your best*—when your ideas flow swiftly and in good order, when your syntax is smooth, your vocabulary accurate. Afterward you think that you couldn't possibly have put things any better than you did.

A first step in achieving that effect is to use only those words and phrases and sentences that you might actually *say* to your reader if you were face-to-face. If you wouldn't say it, if it doesn't *sound* like you, why write it?

The tone of your writing will vary as your readers vary. You would speak more formally to the President of the United States, meeting him for the first time, than to your Uncle Max. For the same reason, a letter to the President would naturally be more formal than a letter to a relative.

But it should still sound like you.

### 11. Strike out words you don't need.

The song goes, "Softly, as in a morning sunrise"—and Ring Lardner explained that this was as opposed to a late afternoon or evening sunrise. Poetic license may be granted for a song, but not for expressions like these:

| **Don't write** | **Write** | |
|---|---|---|
| Advance plan | Plan | |
| Take action | Act | |
| Equally as | Equally | |
| Hold a meeting | Meet | *(continued)* |

15

| Don't write | Write |
|---|---|
| Study in depth | Study |
| New innovations | Innovations |
| Consensus of opinion | Consensus |
| At the present time, at this point in time | Now |
| Until such time as | Until |
| In the majority of instances | In most cases, usually |
| On a local basis | Locally |
| Basically unaware of | Did not know |
| The overall plan | The plan |
| In the area of | Roughly |
| With regard to, in connection with | About |
| In view of, on the basis of | Because |
| In the event of | If |
| For the purpose of, in order to | To |
| Despite the fact that | Although |

## 12. Use current standard English.

A few years ago, a copywriter wrote this sentence in a draft of an advertisement to persuade more people to read *The New York Times:*

> He always acted like he knew what he was talking about.

Musing over the use of "like" in place of "as though" or "as if," someone at *The Times* said: "Yes, I guess that use of 'like' will become standard in five or ten years, but I don't think *The New York Times* should pioneer in these matters." Neither should you. A certain number of your readers will note your "bad English" and find it odious, while the conservative, standard alternative will attract no criticism from anybody. The standard expression is seldom stuffy or in any other way objectionable. If the copywriter had written, "He always acted as if he knew what he was talking about," it would have sounded both natural and literate.

*The rule for "like" is simple: Don't use it in any case where "as if" or "as though" would fit comfortably.*

"Hopefully" is another word whose misuse still annoys many literate people. It is *not* synonymous with "I hope that." It means "in a hopeful manner" or "in a hopeful state of mind," as in:

I opened the envelope hopefully; perhaps it would contain the check I was waiting for.

If you write, "Hopefully, the check will be in the envelope," you are actually saying that the *check* will be sitting there in the envelope in an optimistic state of mind. What you mean is, "I hope the check will be in the envelope."

Nothing will call your literacy into question so promptly as using "I" for "me," or "she" for "her."

Many people, though they have degrees from reputable colleges, make this illiterate mistake: "He asked both Helen and I to go to the convention." Try the pronoun alone. You would never write, "He asked I to go to the convention."

**13. Don't write like a lawyer or a bureaucrat.**

"Re" is legalese meaning "in the matter of" and is never necessary outside formal legal documents. You don't need it

17

in the heading or the title of your paper any more than the Bible needs "RE: GENESIS."

The slash—as in and/or—is bureaucratese. Don't write, "We'll hold the meeting on Monday and/or Tuesday." Write, "We'll hold the meeting on Monday or Tuesday—or on both days, if necessary." Longer—but requires less work from your reader.

**14. Keep in mind what your reader doesn't know.**

Your reader seldom knows ahead of time where you are going or what you are trying to say. Never expect people to read your *mind* as well as your letter or paper.

Take into account how much you can assume your reader knows—what background information, what facts, what technical terms.

Watch your abbreviations. Will they be an indecipherable code to some readers? Might they be ambiguous even to those in the know?

*M is code for a thousand in the United States, for a million in England; 9/12/81 means September 12, 1981, here—December 9 over there.*

If you must use abbreviations like M and MM, define them the first time they appear in your paper. "The cost per thousand (CPM) is a figure that we will keep an eye on throughout this proposal."

**15. Punctuate carefully.**

Proper punctuation functions like road signs, helping your reader to navigate your sentences. A left-out comma, or a comma in the wrong place, can get your reader badly lost, forcing him to backtrack and work through the sentence again.

He didn't agree with the third point and the fourth point made things all the more complicated.

On first reading, the reader may think that the writer didn't agree with either the third *or* fourth point. On reaching "made," he discovers that he's gone wrong. A comma prevents that mistake:

> He didn't agree with the third point, and the fourth point made things all the more complicated.

A common mistake in business writing is to use quotation marks for emphasis: *This bolt will give you "superior" tensile strength.* The head of a tobacco company once put quotation marks around a word in an important paper, and when his administrative assistant asked him why he did that, he replied that it was to stress the truth of the point. The assistant asked whether it would stress the truth if he were to register at a hotel as John Durgin and "wife."

**16. Use facts (and numbers) with restraint.**

Include the principal facts necessary to support your point, and face up to those that weigh against you. But don't throw in unnecessary or irrelevant details.

Don't stretch the facts to support your viewpoint. Don't serve up half-truths to camouflage bad news. Favor simple candor over euphemisms. Intelligent readers develop a nose for cagey writing and are seldom taken in by it.

Never exaggerate. It is more convincing to understate than to overstate. Even a single obvious exaggeration can make your reader suspicious of your entire position. Don't expect your reader to do your toning down for you.

Distinguish between opinion and fact, so that your reader is never in doubt as to which is which.

| **Opinion stated as fact** | **Opinion stated as opinion** |
|---|---|
| The information would be useful, but would cost too much to obtain. | We'd all like to lay our hands on that information, but none of us thinks it's worth what it would cost. |
| We can't get started by May 1. | I doubt if we can get started by May 1. |

Round out numbers conservatively. Don't call 6.7 "nearly seven"—call it "over six and a half."

H. L. Mencken gave an obituary writer a sealed envelope to be opened on Mencken's death. The message: "Don't overdo it."

**17. Write so that you cannot be misunderstood.**

It is not enough to write so that you can be understood. You must eliminate any possibility of *mis*understanding. One can take many a sentence to mean the opposite of what the author intended. Consider this puzzling sentence from a newspaper column:

> ". . . he blames the former U.S. secretary of state, Henry Kissinger, for opposing attempts to forestall the U.S. airlift that prevented the most violent of Mideast wars."

Exactly what is Secretary Kissinger being blamed for—was he in favor of the U.S. airlift or was he against it? What prevented the most violent of Mideast wars—the U.S. airlift or the attempts to forestall it? Such ambiguity often results from a single sentence trying to carry too much cargo. Break up your sentence; it will work wonders. Take this example from a Nuclear Regulatory Commission report:

> "It would be prudent to consider expeditiously the provision of instrumentation that would provide an unam-

20

*biguous indication of the level of fluid in the reactor vessel."*

If you break that idea into two sentences, and follow other suggestions in this chapter, you might end up with something like this:

*We should make up our minds quickly about getting better gauges. Good gauges would tell us exactly how much fluid is in the reactor vessel.*

---

When God wanted to stop the people from building the Tower of Babel, he did not smite them down with a thunderbolt. He said:

*". . . let us go down, and there confound their language, that they may not understand one another's speech."*

He could think of no surer way to foil the project than to garble communications.

# Chapter 3

---

# Business letters and memos that get things done

---

M aster the letter, and you have mastered the most versatile of business tools.

Unlike a telephone call, a letter can be referred to over and over. You can study it, ponder it, make notes on it, pass it on to other people.

Unlike a meeting, it can go with you anywhere.

If you need to refresh your memory on what a letter says, days or years later, there it is—in black and white.

A letter is as private or public as you choose to make it.

A letter is a boon to both writer and reader. It allows the writer to express his ideas with precision. It allows the reader to consider those ideas when and where he chooses.

This chapter covers generalizations that apply to almost any business letter; specific suggestions for particular kinds of letters; and principles governing internal business memos.

# How to write a business letter

## 1. Spell all names right.

On the envelope and in the letter. The names of individuals and of firms and organizations.

A misspelled name gets you off on the wrong foot. It suggests to the reader that you don't care. A sloppy person. Check all names, no matter how much trouble it takes.

Use Mr. or Ms.—many people appreciate a touch of formality and nobody resents it. But leave it out rather than get it wrong when you aren't sure what sex you're writing to, and can't find out. Mickey, Terry, Gerry, Sandy, and many other names come on both girls and boys.

## 2. Get the address right.

Check every detail. Mail addressed incorrectly seems slipshod at best, and at worst doesn't arrive.

Always put a return address on the envelope. The stamp might fall off, or God knows what.

## 3. Think carefully about the salutation.

"Dear" is a convention we're stuck with. Odd and antiquated though it may sound, efforts to avoid it seem artificial, self-conscious, and downright rude.

What comes after "Dear" is worth some thought.

Use first names only when you're already on a first-name basis. Don't become anybody's pen pal by unilateral action.

Use titles—Dr., Judge, Professor, Senator.

An excellent but little-used alternative is to include both first and last names: "Dear Joan Larson." It is less formal than "Dear Ms. Larson," but doesn't presume personal acquaintance—like "Dear Joan."

This is an attractive way to address somebody you have met but who may not remember you. Or somebody important and senior to you whom you know only slightly. Or the other way

23

around: Oscar Hammerstein II, the great songwriter, wrote "Dear Joel Raphaelson" in a letter to Raphaelson, then in college, about a review of *South Pacific* in the college newspaper, and it seemed entirely appropriate, both courteous and cordial.

## 4. Consider beginning with a title.

Many business letters are parts of a long-term correspondence between seller and customer, attorney and client, private firm and government bureau. In such cases, it's a good idea to follow the salutation with a title.

> Dear George:
> Acme legal action: second phase

A title identifies the subject *at a glance,* and is a blessing for anybody who ever has to dig out previous correspondence on it.

Consider using a title even on one-time-only letters to strangers. No other opening so quickly identifies the subject of your letter:

> Dear American Express:
> Lost credit card—Account #3729-051721

## 5. Make your first sentence work hard.

Since titles on letters aren't standard practice, they may strike you as too abrupt or too impersonal for many situations. Then your *first sentence* has to perform the functions of a title. Your reader wants to know *at once* what the letter is about.

There is no need for the written equivalent of small talk. The most courteous thing you can do is spare your reader the trouble of puzzling out what you're getting at.

### Roundabout

Dear Classmate,

As you know, we had a wonderful 15th reunion last June. We can all be proud of the class gift we presented at that time. Now we are well into the first year of the university's '80s campaign and this seems a good time to report on our involvement.

### Straight to the point

Dear Classmate,

It's time to pull together our 16th annual gift to the university. You'll remember we gave a whopper at our 15th reunion—but the need goes on.

What about letters responding to inquiries, or on a subject introduced in previous correspondence? Can you presume that the reader will know what your letter is about, having brought up the subject himself in an earlier letter?

Yes—up to a point. Here are two answers to a request for information:

### Too windy

Dear Mr. Allen:

I am writing in response to your letter of June 24, in which you express an interest in the literature describing our line of herbicides, with particular reference to the control of dandelions in residential lawns. Unfortunately, we are all out of our pamphlets on this subject, but perhaps the following information will be of assistance.

### Too abrupt

Dear Mr. Allen:

I'm sorry that we're out of the literature you asked for. Here's some information that may include what you need.

The letter on the right presumes too much. If Mr. Allen, who may write dozens of letters a day, doesn't happen to remember exactly what he wrote about to this particular firm, days or weeks ago, the first two sentences don't help him. He needs a speedy reminder of his inquiry—more direct than the first letter, less abrupt than the second.

> Dear Mr. Allen:
>
> We've run out of our literature on controlling dandelions. I'm sorry, and I'll send it as soon as a fresh supply gets here. Meanwhile, maybe this information will help.

The short first sentence reminds Mr. Allen of the subject and tells him the chief thing he needs to know.

Always identify your subject in your first sentence.

## 6. Stop when you're through.

Just as some letters take their time to wind up and get going, many slow down before stopping.

Avoid platitudes like these:

> Please call if you have any questions.
>
> I hope this answers your concern.
>
> Please give this matter your careful consideration.

Unless you have something to say that is more than a formality, simply *stop*. If your last sentence says what your reader would assume or do anyway, as in the examples above, leave it out.

Such twaddle doesn't sound sincere or friendly. It sounds like what it is: routine formality. Your ending won't seem abrupt if your tone throughout the letter has been warm and personal.

If you want to add a personal touch, make sure that what you say *is* personal, and something you mean.

I've been reading about your heat wave and wonder how you're getting along.

George, customers like you make this business worthwhile.

### 7. Be specific about next steps.

If you want your letter to lead to action, your last paragraph should make clear what you would like that action to be. Or, if you're taking the action yourself, what you're going to do:

| Vague | Specific |
|-------|----------|
| We're hoping to hear from you soon. | Please let us know your decision by August 1 so that we can meet your deadline. |
| I'm looking forward to getting together with you to talk more. | Are you free for lunch on Friday, July 17? I'll call that morning to confirm. |

### 8. Use an appropriate sign-off.

Gene Shalit, the television personality, signs all his letters "Thine." It's a personal trademark, like his hairstyle. In general, though, your sign-off isn't the place to assert individuality. Keep it conventional and appropriate to your tone.

"Yours truly" benefits from a lack of any specific silly meaning. It is as rooted in convention as "Dear George," and useful for that reason.

"Sincerely" and "Sincerely yours" are all right if you don't mind proclaiming something your reader should take for granted.

So many people have latched on to "Cordially" that we have become numb to its mindless assertion of hearty friendship. Just don't use it on non-cordial letters, e.g., "We've turned your case over to our attorneys. Cordially, . . ."

"Regards," "Best wishes," "All the best" are more personal than the others and less formal, but not appropriate if you don't know your reader.

And there isn't anything wrong with simply signing your name after your last sentence.

## How to handle some common kinds of letters

### Letters that ask for something

Say what you want, right away. Don't start by explaining *why* you want it. Your reader won't be interested in your reasons before you reveal what you're asking for.

Dear Mr. Sullivan:

**Our problem.** ⌈We are a new electronics firm and we need to set up a department to do some basic research.⌊

**Our thinking.** ⌈Accordingly it occurred to our president, Mr. Gene Schultz, that it would be a good idea if we found out how some giant research depart-⌊

**Still hasn't said what we *want*.** ⌈ments such as the Bell Laboratories were organized in the early days.⌊

Don't *start* by expressing your appreciation.

Dear Mr. Sullivan:

I would greatly appreciate your help on a matter in which the Bell Laboratories may be uniquely well informed.

Write that letter like this:

Dear Mr. Sullivan:

**Says what we want, and that we'll pay.** ⌈Do you have any literature that spells out how the Bell Laboratories were organized in the early days? If so, would you send it to me and bill me?⌊

**Explains why.** [We're a small new electronics firm and your early experience might help us figure out the best way to set up our research program.

**Thanks!** [Your help would be invaluable to us.

That's the correct order for letters of inquiry: *first,* what you want; *second,* who you are and why you want it; *third,* an expression of appreciation for favors to come.

If you're asking for routine information—a copy of a published speech, records on your bank account, a price list—you can leave out the reason you want it and shorten your thanks.

## How to say no

No, we don't have a job for you. No, we won't give you more credit. No, we don't agree that it was our fault and that we owe you a refund. No, we can't get your order to you in time for Christmas. No, we won't publish your story. No, we can't contribute to your charity.

Turning somebody down in writing may seem easier than doing it in person, but in some ways it's a lot harder. It is less personal and more permanent.

The reader can't see the expression on your face. Nor can he hear the tone of your voice. Nor can he ask questions on the spot about things that puzzle him or that he takes issue with.

Your letter has to compensate for those disadvantages:

- It must be as *clear* as you would be in person.

- It must be as *tactful* and *understanding* as you would be in person. Pay close attention to your tone.

- You must anticipate your reader's questions and objections and do your best to answer them.

*Put everything in your letter to this test: Would you say it, and would you say it in that way, if you were face-to-face with your reader?*

"We regret to inform you that . . ." is the standard opening of millions of "no" letters. It is hard to imagine anybody ever *saying,* "I regret to inform you that . . ." You'd say, "I know how disappointed you're going to be, but there just isn't any way I can do that" or "No, I don't think that will be possible —but how about this as an alternative?"

Let's say you're the manager of a store that sells refrigerators. After using your top-of-the-line model for almost three years, a customer has reported that it conked out on a hot weekend when she was away, and that she returned to find all her food spoiled.

She wants you to replace the refrigerator with a new one, free, and to charge nothing for the service call that put hers back into commission—only temporarily, she fears.

Here is how some people would respond:

Dear Ms. Traggert:

**An institutional thumbs down.**

I regret to inform you that we are unable to accommodate your request for a new refrigerator. Our repairman reports that the trouble was minor and is unlikely to recur.

**What a dope you were!**

At the time of purchase, you were offered a three-year service contract. Had you accepted it, our service call would have cost you nothing additional.

**Our hands are tied.**

But since you did not accept it, we are required to charge you for the service.

**Boy, do we sound sincere.**

I sincerely regret any inconvenience this episode may have caused you and hope that you will now get many years of satisfactory service out of your Model 6034-Y.

Yours truly,

30

A turndown like this, with its chill, corporate tone, is all but guaranteed to lose a customer for your store.

If you were to hear Ms. Traggert's story at a dinner party, you wouldn't say, "That episode may have been inconvenient for you." You would respond spontaneously with something like, "That's *awful*—what a way to come home from a weekend!" Why not start your letter in the same human way?

> Dear Ms. Traggert:
>
> How terrible for you to come home from a weekend and find all the food in your refrigerator spoiled. I can imagine how you must have felt.

The reader now knows that at least you appreciate her predicament. You might continue in the same vein:

**Agreeing is better than arguing.**

> I quite agree that any refrigerator—and particularly a deluxe model such as yours—should give you trouble-free service for a lot longer than three years.

**Puts problem in perspective.**

> However, no manufacturer's system of quality control is perfect—which is why we advise our customers to invest in a service contract.

**Appeals to reader's sense of fairness. Note use of first person.**

> If I were to charge you nothing for your service call, you would, in effect, be getting the benefits of a service contract without having paid for it.

**Seriously considers reader's request. Gives full reasons for turning it down.**

> In considering your request for us to replace your refrigerator, I have talked to the repairman who fixed it. He assures me that there is nothing fundamentally wrong—the problem was caused by a freak failure of a common bolt, which he has never seen happen before. He feels it is most unlikely to recur: "A million to one against it," he said.

31

| | |
|---|---|
| **Even the turndown is sympathetic.** | I don't think a new refrigerator would be any more likely to give you the years of service you have every right to expect. |
| **Leaves door open.** | But should you have further trouble, I hope you will get in touch with me at once. |

Yours truly,

In this letter, the author shows a personal interest in the woman's situation. He treats her demands as reasonable, and takes the trouble to explain why he is turning them down. He leaves channels of communication open—just in case. In short, his letter sounds as though he cares.

**Never say no in anger**—no matter how angry the other party may be. *You* are in the position of power. Control yourself. Always appreciate the feelings of the person you are turning down.

**Never belittle anybody**—never make him feel as though his request was foolish or unreasonable. Always show consideration for his point of view.

**Never say no casually,** in an offhand manner. Always take the trouble to explain your reasons.

All of this applies just as forcefully to a *form* letter. Do everything you can to make it sound as little like a form letter as possible.

The admissions officers at Princeton turn down nearly nine thousand applicants every year. Here is their sensitive form letter:

Dear Ms.___:

The admission staff has completed its selection of the Princeton Class of 1984, and I am afraid that I must report that we shall not be able to offer you a place.

Since each candidate presented a unique set of credentials, this letter cannot possibly explain the reasons for each decision. Let me assure you, however, that our decisions were not reached quickly or easily and that, because of the highly competitive nature of our admission process, we had to disappoint many applicants who were qualified to do the work at Princeton.

Needless to say, in making our decisions we do not claim to possess either special wisdom or infallible judgment. Because our task has been to select from nearly 11,000 applicants those 2,150 who we think will best comprise a class that is both excellent and diverse, we have had to turn down thousands of talented and interesting people. We have tried to be as fair as possible with all applicants, and our decisions should not be interpreted as judgments passed upon either their innate worth or their ability to contribute to society.

I hope it will not seem out of place if I add here a personal observation about college admissions. The importance of this spring is not that you have been admitted to some universities and colleges and denied admission to others, but rather that you are ending a major portion of your life and beginning another. The years ahead will be filled with academic and personal challenges that can be both frightening and exhilarating, and with those years there will come a new sense of independence and maturity. In the final analysis, it is not primarily the institution you attend but rather your desire to learn from and with other people that will make college an exciting and fulfilling experience.

With best wishes,

Sincerely,

A clear and considerate letter written with sympathy for how the reader is going to feel. That's the secret of how to say no.

## How to collect money owed you

It's hard to write a good collection letter. You don't want to irritate your reader. But you do want to get the money.

**Watch your tone of voice.**

If you're reminding somebody that his payment is a few days overdue, don't sound as though you're about to send your lawyer after him.

| **Bad** | **Better** |
| --- | --- |
| Dear Mr. Jones: | Dear Mr. Jones: |
| It has come to our attention that you have failed to remit your June payment, which became overdue on June 12. | I'm writing to let you know that your June payment (due on June 12) hasn't reached us yet. |

On the other hand, if you *are* going to take legal action, don't pussyfoot around. Come right out and say what you mean:

Dear Mr. Hinson:

Your June payment is now three months overdue. You have not responded to three letters in which I asked if you thought there was an error in the bill. I cannot reach you by telephone.

Therefore I'm asking our lawyers to collect the $104.56 that you owe us.

**Watch your choice of words.**

Never use words which suggest that your reader is a criminal. "Delinquent" is a favorite of righteous bill collectors, as in "You have been delinquent in meeting your payments for two months in a row."

Your object is to get the money owed you; making your reader angry is not likely to send him to his checkbook.

Don't imply that your reader is a *liar*. If a woman has written you that she paid her bill promptly on the first of each of the last four months, and you have received no payments, don't write, "You claim that you paid your bill each month . . ."

The word "claim" reeks of disbelief. If she *is* lying, it won't help. If she *isn't,* it will infuriate her.

Better to take her at her word and suggest a positive next step:

Dear Ms. Bossler:

| | |
|---|---|
| **Assumes truthfulness.** | Although you've been mailing your payments promptly, we have no record of receiving them. |
| **Admits possibility of own error.** | Perhaps the error is in our records. Since you have been paying by check, your bank will by now have returned two and perhaps three of your canceled checks, if in fact we have deposited them. |
| **Suggests constructive action.** | Please look for them and if you find them, send us photocopies at our expense so we can set our records right. |
| **Asks for payment courteously but firmly.** | If you *cannot* find the canceled checks, we must assume the payments somehow got lost. Would you then send us a new check covering at least the first three payments, and preferably all four? |
| **Reduces likelihood of yet another "lost" check.** | I enclose an addressed, stamped envelope. |

Yours truly,

There is nothing in such a letter to irritate an innocent customer; nor is there any loophole for further delay on the part of a guilty one.

Keep in mind that you want to get the money your reader owes you. You don't want to put him down, or anger him, or send him to jail.

## How to complain

Never write just to let off steam. Write to get something done —your money back, or faster service, or a mistake rectified.

Is the person who will read your letter at fault for what went wrong? If not, there's no point in getting sore in your letter. While anger has its place in correspondence as in life, more often than not you'll get better results from a cool, lucid statement of what's gone wrong and what you'd like done about it.

Include *everything* your reader needs to know to take action —account number, item number, pertinent dates, form numbers, photocopies of canceled checks, photocopies of bills.

If you leave anything out, you may have to wait through another round of correspondence before you make progress.

Ask for a reply with a specific statement of what the next step will be:

> Please let me know what action you plan to take, and when.

> If you are not the person who handles this, please get my letter to the right person at once. And please let me know that you've done so, and who it is. I'd appreciate that information by Friday, May 10, at the latest.

Be clear. Be complete—and you can toss in a heartrending description of what you have suffered. Be firm. Be courteous. That's the kind of letter that usually gets the fastest results.

If it fails, raise hell. Write to the head of the organization and include all correspondence. Nine times out of ten you'll get satisfaction from the boss.

## How to answer complaints

Never be defensive. If the complaint is reasonable, say so— and say what you're going to do about it.

Neiman-Marcus, the Dallas-based chain of department stores, has built much of its reputation on its responsiveness to customers. Here is how Chairman Richard Marcus replied to one customer's complaint:

Dear Ms. Klugman:

**Accepts the complaint at face value.** I am astonished to learn of the shoddy service you recently received from our Mail Order Department, and there is no excuse for the lack of response and discourteous conversation you had with a member of our Mail Order phone staff.

**Says what he's going to do about it.** I'm asking Mr. Ron Foppen, senior vice-president and director of our Mail Order operation, to investigate this matter immediately, and he will personally contact you within a few days.

**Apologizes.** I apologize for any inconvenience and embarrassment we may have caused you,

**Asks for continued business.** and trust that we will have the opportunity of serving you better in the future.

Yours sincerely,
Richard Marcus

Far from being defensive, Mr. Marcus comes right out and calls the store's service "shoddy" and says that "there is no excuse" for it.

The entire letter is personal, sympathetic and responsive.

What if you feel that the complaint lacks any justification? Say so, but be courteous.

Intelligent readers are good at detecting the slightest hint of irritability or impatience. You should be at least as courteous on paper as you would be in person. Forthright and direct. Never sarcastic or rude.

## When to use very short letters

A short letter—sometimes no longer than a sentence or two —can be highly effective.

It can establish your interest.

> Dear Mr. Woodrow:
>
> Your proposal interests us a lot. We'll get back to you as soon as we've sorted out our budget problems for next year—no later than the end of next week.

It can let your reader know what's happening, and demonstrate your thoroughness.

> Dear Ms. Pruitt:
>
> Half your shipment went out this morning, air express. The other half follows next Monday, parcel post, as you requested.

It can say thank you.

> Dear Helen:
>
> I hope you can keep Dan Murphy on our account forever. He's the best sales representative I've ever dealt with.

## How to write a memorandum

Memos are letters to people within your organization, or to people outside it with whom you work closely.

Like good letters, good memos go directly to the point. Write in a personal tone. After all, you are writing to *colleagues*.

From a purely selfish point of view, you should take even more care with memos than with letters. When a confusing or ambiguous memo slows things down, or messes them up, the bad results are within your own organization.

There is another reason.

*If the reading time of every memo could be shortened by as little as twenty seconds, even a small firm could save hours every week and days every year.*

Here are specific suggestions for the *format* of memos, and on how to handle certain *kinds* of memos.

**1. Put a title on every memo.**

Your title should never be clever or tricky. It should identify —swiftly, and for all readers—what your memo is about.

A memo proposing an overdue raise for Tony Andrino should not be titled LONG OVERDUE—title it RAISE FOR TONY ANDRINO.

If you are responding to somebody else's memo, say so in your title:

FRANK OWEN'S JUNE 22 MEMO ON HOG PRICES

SEX-BLIND ADMISSIONS:
YOUR NOVEL IDEAS (MAY 3)

Don't worry about the length of your title—say as much as necessary to identify your subject:

POLLUTED RIVERS—MAJOR DIFFERENCE
BETWEEN COLORADO AND WYOMING

Center your title in capital letters over your message. It's easier for someone to spot there, thumbing through files or briefcase, than tucked off to the left along with the list of addressees.

**2. List names alphabetically.**

If you list the people getting your memo in order of importance, you often run into complications. Is the head of manufacturing more important than the head of research? Who comes first among four assistant deans?

Such problems evaporate if you put *all* names in alphabetical order, except when that would be ludicrous. It would be ludicrous, for example, in a memo to the personnel director with copies to eight secretaries and the president, to list the president alphabetically among the secretaries. Put the president's name first; list the secretaries alphabetically.

## 3. Address memos only to the person who must take action.

Send copies to the people you merely want to keep informed.

| From: William Durwin | cc: Cindy Lee |
| To: Margaret Baker | Bob Nieman |
| | Sam Nasikawa |

This says that Mr. Durwin wants Ms. Baker to *do* something, and the others just to know what's going on.

If *several* people must do something, address the memo to all of them and make clear what each must do.

## 4. Make your structure obvious.

Before you start to write, decide on structure. It will depend on the length, complexity, and nature of your subject.

Any memo longer than half a page requires a structure—*and the structure should be apparent to your reader.* Otherwise your memo will seem to ramble. Your reader will have a hard time remembering your points and how they hang together.

If what you want to say falls into conventional outline form —for instance, three main points, each supported by several examples, with a comment or two on each example—your outline will serve as your structure.

A clear structure helps your reader to remember your points. It also makes your memo easy to refer to.

Some memos are actually complex reports or recommendations, running a half-dozen pages or more. In any such memo, start by outlining what you're going to cover.

This memo is divided into three sections:

- The problem.
- Four possible solutions.
- My recommendation.

Or write a brief *covering memo* and attach your report or plan as a separate document. This works well for major papers.

One useful structure is often overlooked: *a simple series of numbered points.* It has many advantages:

1. It suits your purpose exactly when you wish to make a number of loosely related observations on a single subject.

2. It eliminates the need to write connectives. When you're finished with one point, you plunge directly into the next.

3. It organizes your thoughts visually for your reader.

4. Your numbered sections can be as long or short as you wish. Some can be a single sentence, others two or more paragraphs.

   All that matters is that each number should indicate the start of a new and distinct thought.

5. The numbers make your memo easy to refer to.

**5. End with a call to action.**

Say what you expect to happen as a result of your memo. Exactly what must now be done, by whom, and by when. Be specific.

If your memo raises questions, ask for answers by a specific date.

If your memo replies to questions raised by somebody else, simply stop when you're finished. Don't waste your reader's time with such homilies as "I hope this answers your questions." Since it goes without saying that you hope you've answered them, go without saying it.

If your memo is a report, draw conclusions from what you saw or heard or found out. Specify how certain you feel about your conclusions. Some will be beyond question, others purely speculative. Tell your reader which are which.

## 6. Send handwritten notes.

Brief memos written by hand save time and by their nature are more personal and direct. Praise and appreciation can be specially effective in handwriting:

> George:
> That's sensational news about acme. Get some rest now — you deserve it !

> Susan:
> Your report is _superb_. I'll react to your recommendations as soon as I get back from Fargo.

Since handwriting is personal, make sure whatever you write *sounds* personal.

## 7. Be careful with humor—or anger.

Don't try to be funny in memos unless you are *positive* that *all* your readers will get the joke. That includes people who may not be on your list, but might see a copy.

Avoid irony or sarcasm. Somebody will take it straight and get upset. People can brood for days over an innocently intended sentence or two.

As for anger, when you get angry in person you leave nothing behind other than the *memory* of your anger. When you put it in writing, you leave a *permanent record.* You may be sorry about that—after you cool down.

Angry memos do have their place. A good rule is to *write* it when you're angry, but don't *send* it until the next day, when you have cooled off enough to reflect on the consequences.

## 8. Should it be a memo at all?

Could you handle it faster and more efficiently on the telephone? Or by dropping in to somebody's office?

An Italian proverb says: "Think much, speak little, write less."

The world is suffocating in paper. Often the kindest thing you can do for your reader is to give him nothing more to read at all.

I have crossed out on the attached paper many unsuitable names. Operations in which large numbers of men may lose their lives ought not to be described by code-words which imply a boastful and overconfident sentiment, such as "Triumphant," or, conversely, which are calculated to invest the plan with an air of despondency, such as "Woebetide," "Massacre," "Jumble," "Trouble," "Fidget," "Flimsy," "Pathetic," and "Jaundice." They ought not to be names of a frivolous character, such as "Bunnyhug," "Billingsgate," "Aperitif," and "Ballyhoo." They should not be ordinary words often used in other connections, such as "Flood," "Smooth," "Sudden," "Supreme," "Full-force," and "Fullspeed." Names of living people -- Ministers or Commanders -- should be avoided; e.g., "Bracken."

2.  After all, the world is wide, and intelligent thought will readily supply an unlimited number of well-sounding names which do not suggest the character of the operation or disparage it in any way and do not enable some widow or mother to say that her son was killed in an operation called "Bunnyhug" or "Ballyhoo."

3.  Proper names are good in this field. The heroes of antiquity, figures from Greek and Roman mythology, the constellations and stars, famous racehorses, names of British and American war heroes, could be used, provided they fall within the rules above. There are no doubt many other themes that could be suggested.

4.  Care should be taken in all this process. An efficient and a successful administration manifests itself equally in small as in great matters.

*Churchill's memos got into the subject fast.*

# Chapter 4

---

# How to get
# people to send you money

---

Think of your mail at home. Some magazines. Maybe an invitation. Several announcements—a sale, a new restaurant, a concert series. A catalog or two. Bills. An appeal for contributions to a candidate for public office or to a charity.

People asking for *money.*

Less and less do we correspond with friends and family; now we telephone. More and more of our mail comes from strangers asking for money. Sooner or later, someone will ask *you* to write one of those letters.

The two kinds of letters you are most likely to be asked to write are *sales letters* and *fund-raising letters*—subjects about which books have been written. Here are some of the things professionals do to get people to part with their money.

## The first principle: test.

Direct mail is mail that asks the reader to send money *directly* to the writer or organization, rather than to go to a store. It is a science, measurable and accountable. You count the money that comes in the mail, and you know how you've done.

Which leads to the first principle. *Test.*

It is common to find that one mailing will produce five times the response of another. Differences of 19-to-1 are not unheard of.

You don't have to be big to test. There are inexpensive ways. It pays to test if you plan to repeat your mailing from time to time, or to send it to a substantial number of people.

Don't assume anything. You will be surprised.

- People will read *long* letters. They often pull better than short ones.

- Some months (or even weeks or days) are more productive than others for some kinds of mailings.

- Sometimes people will respond better to a higher price than to a lower one—if it is more believable.

- People will respond again and again to the identical mailing. Don't change for the sake of change. You should never change a successful mailing until you have a *proven* winner to replace it.

*Important*—it's best to test only one change at a time. If you test several, you won't know which helped, or how much.

If you *cannot* test, take advantage of the testing of others. When you receive the same mailing over and over, year after year, you can be reasonably sure it has been proven in testing. Study it.

## The second principle: estimate how much you will get.

To decide how much to *invest* in each potential customer, you must know or estimate how much each customer is *worth.*

If you expect people to send money just once, the calculation is easy. Will you get back enough money to cover the cost of the mailing plus the cost of merchandise—and leave you a profit? If yes, go ahead. If no, start again.

Most direct mail is in a different category—it goes to people who may buy *more than once:*

- Customers whose repeat orders you can reasonably expect.

- Subscribers—to magazines, book clubs, record clubs, art clubs—who are likely to renew their subscriptions or send in new orders.

- Contributors to schools or hospitals or the United Way or any other cause or charity, who might well give again in future years.

For this kind of response, you can invest more in your initial mailing—even if it loses money the first time around, as it often does.

# What works best in sales letters

Here are some tips from the professionals:

### 1. Have a strategy.

A sales letter is an advertisement delivered in the mail. Successful advertising starts with clear thinking on *what* to say— and to *whom.*

Try to form a picture of your prospect—in terms of age and income, life-style, attitudes, what products he uses.

Then determine the single most important benefit your product offers. Products and services provide lots of benefits, but one must be more important than the others. The essence of a strategy is sacrifice; you must play down the lesser benefits to concentrate on the biggest.

## 2. Project a personality.

Sometimes the *tone* of your letter can be as important as what you say. Do you want to project an aura of high quality, or a sense of urgency, or good value, or what?

## 3. Make sure the offer is right.

The professional direct-mail writer works on the coupon first —not the letter. What is the offer? How should it be stated? What are the terms?

The offer is what gets the action.

It may be a reduced price, a premium, a charter subscription, a ten-day free-trial offer or a combination of these.

> The National Audubon Society offers a membership package of outings, bird walks, workshops, films, lectures, discounts on books and stamps and prints, and a subscription to *Audubon Magazine.* All for annual dues of $18.

Small changes in an offer, or even in the way the offer is presented, can make an immense difference in response. The *Economist* magazine tested five special offers against its standard subscription terms:

**a.** $65 for 56 weeks

**b.** $42.50 for 39 weeks

**c.** $29.95 for 39 weeks

**d.** Free trial

**e.** Pick your own terms from these options

The results are confidential. But they astonished most of the insiders—and saved the *Economist* a lot of money.

## 4. Get people to open the envelope.

If the sales letter is an advertisement, the envelope is the headline, serving to attract the reader to read on.

Always *say* something on your envelope. Here are some envelope-openers on successful mailings:

ADVANCE NOTICE

PLEASE OPEN AT ONCE:
DATED MATERIALS INSIDE

R.S.V.P.

WE HAVE A FREE GIFT FOR YOU
(DETAILS INSIDE)

RECEIVE FOUR FREE ISSUES

No matter how terrific a letter you've written, it does no good in an unopened envelope in the wastebasket.

## 5. Start fast.

You can't afford a leisurely warm-up before throwing your first pitch. Open your letter with an idea that will make your reader say, "This sounds interesting. I'd like to know more about it."

> Dear Friend of the Met:
> How would you like to attend a private dress rehearsal at the Metropolitan Opera House—a special privilege limited to "insiders" only?

> Dear Tennis Camper:
> "Where was he ten years ago?" laments Arthur Ashe. And Roscoe Tanner agrees fervently, "Whenever I work with Henry, my game responds one hundred percent."

*Involve* your reader in your first sentence, or your second sentence may never be read.

## 6. Favor long letters over short ones.

Most amateurs assume that people won't read long letters.
The fact is that long letters sell *better* than short ones *if:*

49

- You have an attractive offer.
- You get the reader's attention at the beginning.
- Your letter is loaded with *facts.*

Look at the mass mailings you receive. How many are just one page? Most include several pieces of literature *and* a letter several pages long.

There is no mystery to the success of long letters. You are asking your reader to make an *investment*—in time, money, or both. You must *convince* her that what you're selling is worth it.

> Publishers Clearing House—one of the largest and most successful direct marketing companies —sends a well-tested mailing package that includes six enclosures plus a letter almost 1,000 words long.

Remember that your reader is looking for *information,* not for reading pleasure. Every sentence must work for its living.

## 7. Give something away.

You'll be amazed how something free, however small, can add to the power of a sales letter. You can offer a free first copy, special discounts, a free membership certificate, a free pin, free trials.

A simple pamphlet, perhaps one you've already printed for another purpose, can be an effective free offer—and a cheap one.

## 8. Make it inviting to read.

People won't read long letters that *look* formidable, with solid blocks of text.

Use visual devices to make your letter look inviting and interesting, easy to get through. (See Chapter 8.)

Think beyond standard envelopes and standard sizes of

paper. The most effective mail is often an *unusual* size. People's curiosity is piqued by varying sizes, shapes and colors.

Generally, the more pieces of paper, the better—provided you have something to say that's important to the reader.

### 9. Make it look like the real thing.

Letters should look like letters, not like advertisements.

Coupons should look like money, certificates like college diplomas or high-grade bonds.

The more genuine it looks, the better it works.

### 10. Give your reader something to do.

Don't let your reader nod in agreement, but do nothing. Your enemy is inertia.

Use simple devices like asking your reader to paste on stickers, to check a preference, or to answer a short quiz. A reader who starts to *do* something with your mailing is a good bet to end up buying.

### 11. Don't let your reader off the hook.

People procrastinate. You must create a reason for your prospect to *act now.*

> The allocation of Collectors Edition Sets makes it necessary to accept reservations on a "first come, first served" basis . . . and under no circumstances can reservations be accepted if postmarked after August 30.

> Why not send the application and deposit in now? We expect the courses to be filled fast, so don't delay.

Danny Newman, America's most successful seller of subscriptions to cultural events, builds all his mailings to a single injunction: SUBSCRIBE NOW.

The close is crucial. Most of your orders will come from people who act right away.

51

**P.S. Try a postscript.**

Many successful letters use a P.S.—to remind the reader of some important detail, to restate the offer, to create a sense of urgency with a deadline or a special premium.

> P.S. I've touched on this before, but I know tennis players, so let me emphasize it: You'll get all the tennis you can sop up. Even during the evening (if you're up to it)—the courts are available for free play.

> P.S. I've also been asked to tell you that because of the limited printing of the premiere issue, we may not be able to send additional first issues, or accept Charter Subscriptions, after April 15.

Why not try a P.S.? It doesn't cost any more. Since so many professionals do it, you can bet they have proved it works.

## What works best in fund-raising letters

In the world of political fund raising by mail, two acknowledged masters are Richard Viguerie, a conservative, and Roger Craver, a liberal. Craver disagrees with Viguerie on every issue, observes *The New York Times,* "except on how to write a letter."

> *"You need a letter filled with ideas and passion," says Craver. "It does not beat around the bush, it is not academic, it is not objective. The toughest thing is to get the envelope open. The next toughest thing is to get the person to read the letter."*

A Craver letter for Handgun Control carries this message on the envelope:

> ENCLOSED: Your first chance to tell the National Rifle Association to go to hell!

The letter starts:

Dear Potential Handgun Victim:

To raise money for charitable, educational or political causes, you must appeal to the *emotions.* People can have strong feelings about a community fund or a church or a candidate. They can *want* to give.

Yet those new to fund raising are often hesitant about asking for money.

The first truth to remember when raising funds is this: Most people don't give *because nobody asked.* Which leads to this rule —*never ask anybody for money until you have given yourself.*

When *you* have given—and given until it hurts—you feel comfortable about asking others; your appeal rings true. You won't feel uneasy about soliciting from anybody, no matter how much money you're asking for.

Direct mail is a growing source of funds for charitable institutions. Few people today seem to have the time to do the door-to-door canvassing on which so many drives used to depend. Fund raisers have discovered the effectiveness of sophisticated mailing programs.

George McGovern financed his presidential candidacy through a committed following and an unprecedented direct-mail campaign, conducted by professionals. One exceptionally effective mailing recognized that most money in election campaigns comes in too late to be of real value.

The strategy was to get funds *early* from McGovern loyalists. The opening line of the letter spoke directly to them:

*"Senator McGovern has asked me to express his deepest thanks to you for the part you played in his great victory in Miami."*

The request took an unusual form—please send four checks to Senator McGovern, dated one month apart. This let the contributor make a commitment *now* without spending the money all at once. It enabled the McGovern people to sign up for valuable television time well in advance.

The letter was six pages long. It made the full case for McGovern. It offered a sterling silver lapel pin as a premium to stimulate action.

> *The result: an unprecedented 25 percent response rate, an average gift of $40, and over $1 million in early campaign funds.*

Which leads to a few more basic rules.

**1. Write first to previous donors.**

People who have given previously are the best source of funds. They need only an inexpensive reminder to prompt their generosity and loyalty.

> The New York Red Cross sends a simple reminder card to previous donors, thanking them for their support. The response rate is 15 percent. The cost is minimal.

You can go back to donors several times and many of them will give several times. You can go to them on a regular schedule or on special occasions, like emergencies. Donors are believers—*and believers give.*

**2. Invest in getting new prospects.**

Because a donor who gives once is likely to give again, it pays to invest heavily in getting a *new* donor.

> New Yorkers who give to the Red Cross typically give seven times in ten years—and increase their gift 20 percent during this period. The true value of a donor is not the initial $7 average, but closer to $60.

With this knowledge, the Red Cross can afford to offer an expensive first aid manual—free—to prospects. The mailing does not pay for itself with the first donation; it does over the years.

## 3. Tell the prospect how much money you want.

The reader does not know how much you expect. Suggesting the amount is up to you.

Do it discreetly. One effective way is to tell people what their money will buy, as the Red Cross does:

> $100— three meals a day for 20 people.
>
> $ 50— training of a volunteer to be a swimming or lifesaving instructor.
>
> $ 35— clothing for one child.
>
> $ 25— training a family member to care for the ill, injured or handicapped at home.
>
> $ 10— shelter for one night for a homeless victim of a fire.

Don't forget to tell people how little you spend on administration. Assure them that you mean it when you say that no contribution is too small, even a dollar.

## 4. Make it emotional.

People don't give to institutions; they give to other people. Put your appeal in personal terms. Use emotion.

> The North Shore Animal League raises over $5 million a year. The envelope message: "WOULD YOU GIVE A DOLLAR—JUST $1.00—TO SAVE A PUPPY'S LIFE?"

Use your letter to give information as well as to get money. Describe the work your organization is doing and say why it is important. Use case histories.

Tell readers what you cannot do—*unless they give.* Don't let them assume that the drive will be successful whether or not they give. Close with a personal and urgent appeal.

## 5. Make your donors members, not just givers.

An effective fund-raising letter gets people to identify with your cause. It makes them feel part of it.

Treat your donors as insiders who care. Send membership certificates and service pins. Send progress reports. Write to say thanks. Thanks, *and won't you give again?*

———

Raising money by mail is a craft, not an art, developed by trial and error.

You can test appeals, premiums, letters, even different envelopes. You can test different mailing lists—by zip code or income or product usage or whatever.

You can use the research and expertise of others by borrowing from mailings that made you want to buy something, or that you have received many times—a sure clue that they are working.

Finding your own winner pays. You save time and money when you repeat it year after year. You can expand it, with testing, to new lists.

Never succumb to the feeling that you are doing something vulgar. Remember Samuel Johnson's ringing declaration: "No man but a blockhead ever wrote for anything but money."

# Chapter 5

---

# How to organize plans and reports

---

T he best report ever written may have been Julius Caesar's *Veni, vidi, vici.*

   *I came, I saw, I conquered.*

Some reports, like Caesar's, describe the outcome of an operation. Most say *what's happened so far and where things stand.*
   A plan states *what to do.*
   The consequences of faulty organization and careless writing are severe. Reports land in wastebaskets, unread. Plans go
straight to the files, unacted on.

## How to write a plan

"For Montgomery," wrote the biographer of the British field
marshal, "it was all a question of having a plan. Once you had
decided what you wanted—what, in military terms, was your
aim—you made a plan, which you then implemented carefully
by stages, maintaining the aim and concentrating all your
resources to achieving it."

Whether you are writing a battle plan or a long-term strategic plan or an annual business plan or a reorganization plan, your objective is the same: *action*.

## 1. State your goal.

A plan should have a goal specific enough so that progress toward it can be measured.

Everything in your plan should pertain to reaching your goal. Cut out all irrelevancies.

## 2. Summarize all pertinent facts.

Include sales, trends, performance against budget, past successes and failures, data about personnel, economic and political considerations. Cover everything that bears on a decision.

## 3. Draw principles from your facts.

You can almost always infer one or more principles from the facts—lessons learned, either from the situation at hand or from others with analogous facts.

Show how facts *fit;* never parade them on their own.

## 4. State the steps you propose to take—and your reasons.

A plan is a recommendation until it is approved. Then it becomes a commitment to action. It describes, step by step, exactly what is supposed to be done.

It covers the reasons for each step. It tells how each step moves toward your goal.

## 5. Anticipate objections.

Any good plan considers alternatives and risks. It anticipates questions and answers them.

Don't cover up problems. Face them squarely. This makes your proposal realistic—and makes *you* realistic. "I never promised you a rose garden."

## A model plan

*America's New Beginning: A Program for Economic Recovery* is the title of President Reagan's controversial program to recast the Federal budget.

The Introduction quickly puts the plan in perspective.

*"This budget plan is one of several parts of the President's overall plan for economic recovery."*

The other parts are summarized: a reduction in individual tax rates, modified depreciation schedules for plant and equipment, a regulatory reform program, a new monetary policy.

It then provides a sweeping overview of goals, proposed steps and benefits.

*"The budget reform plan outlines a comprehensive, multi-year program for ending the recent unsustainable upward spiral of Federal spending and borrowing. It is an essential cornerstone of the President's overall economic program. Its full implementation is crucial to achieving a sustained reduction in inflation and interest rates, and to restoring financial stability to the U.S. economy."*

Eight major features of the plan are then outlined in short paragraphs.

If the reader went no further, the dimensions of this bold and complex plan would be clear. No surprise endings.

The elements of the plan follow, in logical order.

- Historical setting.
- Preliminary budget outlook.
- Receipts with tax-reduction program.
- Currently estimated budget outlook with the President's budget savings and tax-reduction programs.
- New priorities.
- Budget reform criteria.

59

- Program proposals (by agency).
- Summary tables (including economic assumptions and savings by agency).

Pie charts, graphs and statistical tables help the reader through the 209-page document.

There is no larger plan than the Federal budget, and few that approach its complexity—or implications for its citizens and the rest of the world. Whether or not you approve of the Reagan program, it is a good presentation of goals and actions. The principles illustrated by a plan to spend over $600 billion can help you draft any plan you may have to put together.

## How to write a report

Reports cover events large and small—meetings, trips, analyses of competition, developments, good news, bad news.

Some reports aid the planning process; some come after it, reporting on progress or results. Good ones obey the following principles.

### 1. Involve your reader.

Why are you writing the report, and *why should anybody care?* Remember the reader, laden with bulging briefcase.

Good reports get the reader's interest in the first sentence:

> This reports on a management meeting at which a new salary policy was decided.

> The purpose of this report is to assess new competition—a product that could cut our sales in half.

You must command attention before you ask for action.

### 2. Separate opinion from fact.

Both are important, but you must make clear to your reader which is which.

Facts are facts. Conclusions and recommendations are always *opinion.*

How you *choose* facts, and how you marshal them, may well reflect your opinion. You are usually advocating a point of view. But your report will stand up better, especially should it come under fire, if you make a conscious effort not to lump your facts and your opinions into a single undifferentiated pile.

### 3. State the facts fully and accurately.

Newspaper reporters are trained to do this with the famous five Ws—who, what, when, where, why (or how). Not a bad discipline for a writer of reports—who is, literally, a reporter.

> The major findings are that Homebrand sales are off 28 percent, distribution is down 20 percent, and Alien's new product is being purchased by nearly half of all heavy users.

All the facts, unpleasant as well as pleasant.

Never inflate the validity of your facts. If you only visited ten stores in two cities, say so.

### 4. Interpret the facts.

What conclusions do you draw from the facts? What principles can you relate them to? What action do they suggest?

Some reports are purely for the record. Others—the most important ones—are designed to get action.

### 5. Give your report a structure.

Whether you start with a recommendation which you then support with facts, or lay out the facts before making your recommendation, your reader should know *where you are going.*

Here is a structure that often works:

> *Purpose*—why the reader should pay attention.
> *Summary*—no surprise endings.

61

*Findings*—what facts can you marshal?
*Conclusions*—what patterns do you see?
*Recommendations*—what action do you propose?

Each section should be labeled clearly.

## 6. Make it short.

There is no need to parade *all* your information unless the reader needs every detail to understand your report.

Put only essential facts into the body of your report. Relegate charts and supporting data to an appendix.

## 7. Keep its purpose in mind.

There are many kinds of reports with many kinds of purposes.

A *conference report,* for example, has only one purpose: to record decisions taken at meetings. It does not restate arguments or report praise or blame.

It records what was shown or discussed. What was decided (not why). What action is required and who will be responsible for it. When it is due. What money was authorized. It covers actions and decisions—nothing else.

A *competitive report* covers competitive activity, a *progress report* covers progress, and so on.

## 8. Always take notes.

Never trust your memory when collecting material for a report. Write down everything you want to remember.

> *"The horror of that moment," the King went on, "I shall never, <u>never</u> forget!"*
>
> *"You will, though," the Queen said, "if you don't make a memorandum of it."*
>
> Alice's Adventures in Wonderland

The best reports are written by people who take the best notes.

### 9. See for yourself.

A field trip often gives you better answers than any amount of statistics. Or it can lead you to the right questions to ask back in the office.

Generals often go to the front—a personal visit gives them a feeling for what's going on, against which to judge the facts.

Field trips are often a source of ideas. Just as important, they add the breath of life to your reports. An intelligent appraisal of actual conditions can be essential to progress. Report what is happening out there, and what you think should be done about it.

## A model report

The report of the President's Commission on the accident at the Three Mile Island nuclear plant in 1979 bears study as a model of how to write a report.

The event had complex political, legal, economic and technological implications—all of which were faced in a 201-page report that set a direction for the nuclear industry.

Before you even open the report, you learn the commission's chief conclusion. The subtitle is "The Need for Change: The Legacy of TMI."

There will be no call to tear down nuclear plants, nor a soothing dismissal of the warnings. The message is clear: Nuclear power is OK, the systems are not.

A preface outlines the President's charge to the commission, and what the commissioners did to fulfill it.

> *"The purpose of the Commission is to conduct a comprehensive study and investigation of the recent accident involving the nuclear power facility on Three Mile Island in Pennsylvania . . . [including] appropriate recommendations based upon the Commission's findings."*

The preface also specifies what limits the commission worked within. It makes clear that the investigation was "centered on one accident at one nuclear power plant in the United States." The reader can then read the entire 201-page printed report or go directly to the "Overview," with this central conclusion:

> *"To prevent nuclear accidents as serious as Three Mile Island, fundamental changes will be necessary in the organization, procedures, and practices—and above all —in the attitudes of the Nuclear Regulatory Commission and, to the extent that the institutions we investigated are typical, of the nuclear industry."*

The overview prepares the reader for the heart of the report —a discussion of *findings on each subject listed in the President's charge.*

- Assessment of significant events.
- Health effects.
- Public health.
- Emergency response.
- The utility and its suppliers.
- Training of operating personnel.
- The Nuclear Regulatory Commission.
- The public's right to information.

The findings lead to the *recommendations,* covering the same subjects. Views of individual commissioners who dissented from one or more of the recommendations—hardly surprising with so complex and controversial a subject—are listed under *Supplemental Views.*

The report includes an "Account of the Accident," which starts:

> *"On Wednesday, March 28, 1979, 36 seconds after the hour of 4:00 A.M., several water pumps stopped working in the Unit 2 nuclear power plant on Three Mile Island, 10 miles southeast of Harrisburg, Pennsylvania. Thus began the accident at Three Mile Island. In the minutes,*

*hours and days that followed, a series of events—compounded by equipment failures, inappropriate procedures, and human errors and ignorance—escalated into the worst crisis yet experienced by the nation's nuclear power industry.*"

The account is vividly written and illustrated to make events clear to the layman. It takes the reader through the six days of the crisis, day by day, with charts, maps and photographs.

The report concludes with the details that a student of the accident may require—the President's memorandum, the commission's operations and methodology, biographies, staff list and a glossary.

Not every business crisis involves a presidential commission. Nor is every government report a model of good writing. But writers of business reports can learn from this particular commission about how to organize an effective report on a complex and important subject.

# Chapter 6

---

# Add force to speeches and presentations

---

Something seems to come over a person when he writes for an AUDIENCE. He pictures himself behind that podium, and what comes out doesn't sound like anything he'd ever actually *say* to anybody.

Or worse, he can't even get started and sits there staring at a blank sheet of paper.

Author Tom Wolfe reports a dramatic example of freezing at the prospect of writing for an audience. It happened to be an audience for a story, not for a speech, but there was no difference in the effect on Wolfe. *Esquire* magazine had asked him to write about the makers of custom cars in California—an early '60s phenomenon—and he just couldn't get started.

When the deadline approached—and still not even a *beginning*—the managing editor, Byron Dobell, instructed Wolfe to type out his notes for another writer to turn into the story. Wolfe found himself typing those notes as a personal letter to Dobell. He put down "Dear Byron"—and then something happened.

Says Wolfe: "Words started pouring out, without my thinking of literary forms. I was writing for *one guy.*"

Dobell crossed off "Dear Byron," put the notes without change into *Esquire,* and Wolfe had found his voice as a writer.

Addressing "one guy" rather than a faceless audience is a helpful principle to keep in mind when you write a speech or a presentation. Your audience will be listening one person at a time. What you write should sound exactly like *you* talking to *somebody.*

The most effective speeches and presentations sound as if they have been spoken, ad-lib, and not written down at all. Great presenters and speakers make it all sound so easy and so natural that one assumes it just pours out of them. It almost never does.

The good ones write everything down. And they *rehearse*— over and over—revising and revising until everything sounds entirely natural. That should be your goal whenever you write something to be spoken.

## How to write a presentation

The purpose of a presentation is to sell—to persuade people to buy a line of products, hire a firm, undertake a project.

Incompetent, mumbling presentations waste time, bore the audience and fail to persuade.

Some principles for writing persuasive presentations:

### 1. Know your audience.

Don't fly blind. Try to get briefed on everybody you'll be talking to. Anticipate what they will be thinking.

If you use a presentation many times, don't repeat it without *some* change. Each audience is different, and has special interests. Take them into account.

**2. Start with specific, written objectives.**

Everything you say, everything you show, every device you use must move you toward your objectives.

Almost everyone has been to big show-biz presentations at which the entertainment overwhelms the sales message.

Keep things simple. Keep them on target.

**3. Open with a headline stating your theme.**

You need a theme to give your presentation unity and direction. Make it a simple theme, easy to remember, and open with it.

DOUBLE YOUR SALES

CUT YOUR COSTS

NEEDED: A NEW BALL PARK

MORE FUN FOR BOSTONIANS

Tie every element in your presentation to your theme.

**4. Show an agenda.**

Tell your audience what you are going to cover, all your major points.

Describe the structure of your presentation, and say how long it will take. Estimate time conservatively—err on the long side rather than the short side.

> A presentation that is promised for 20 minutes and goes 25 seems like an eternity. The same thing promised for 30 minutes seems short in 25, crisp and businesslike.

Throughout the meeting, refer to the agenda—and your theme—to keep your audience on track.

**5. Talk about your audience, not about yourself.**

While you are talking about *your* credentials and *your* achievements, the people in the audience are thinking about *their* organization, *their* business, *their* problems.

Relate what you offer to your audience's needs. Present everything possible in terms of *benefits to the audience.*

Try to use their organization's name more often than your own.

## 6. Use your imagination.

Look for creative visual devices—interesting ways to present dry, routine materials.

> *Pie charts and bar charts are more interesting than columns of bare numbers. Symbols can be even better—for example, increasingly large pictures of a company's headquarters building to indicate growth of earnings.*

Newsmagazines hire top artists to make their charts interesting and clear. Study their techniques—and borrow from them.

Think of ways to involve your audience. Play games with them. Invite your audience to guess the answers to questions, or to predict the results of research—before you reveal them.

## 7. Do everything that's been asked—and a little more.

Be precise in covering what was requested. If you *cannot* cover some point or other, say so and say why.

Try to add something extra, something *unexpected.* It demonstrates more than routine interest. Play tape recordings of customers describing your audience's product. Quote a speech your audience's chief executive made five years ago.

## 8. Use numbers and headings to guide your audience.

Number your main points on charts or slides, and tell people how many you have.

69

Head each new section to help your audience follow you.

> **Strategy**
>
> **1.** Small markets before big ones.
>
> **2.** Three new markets every six months.
>
> **3.** Concentrate building in spring and summer.

## 9. Prepare for questions.

As you're writing, be alert to your inevitable weak spots.

What are the holes in your argument? What alternatives did you consider? What prejudices does your audience bring to the meeting?

If you cannot build the answers into your presentation, be ready to handle them—briefly and respectfully, so the questioner will feel smart to have asked.

## 10. Finish with a bang.

Don't let a meeting drift off into trivia.

Look for a memorable, dramatic close—something visual, a restatement of your theme, a small gift that symbolizes your main point. "Oh, give me something to remember you by" goes the song. As soon as you've gone, your audience is likely to turn its attention to other things—perhaps to presentations competitive to yours. Leave something to remember you by.

## How to use visual aids

Slides or charts?

Big meetings almost always require big screens—and therefore slides. If you're more than 12 feet from your audience, it is hard to get charts big enough to be read.

70

If you have the choice, think it over carefully.

Slides are seductive. Dramatic photographs, big type, color —all relatively cheap.

Charts are harder to handle. They are not so colorful or dramatic. They often cost more.

*But beware!* Slides require you to turn down the lights, focusing attention on the screen rather than on you, and giving the meeting a formal tone.

People are interested in people. It often pays to keep the lights on and work with charts. The audience then gets to know you.

Slides or charts, follow these rules:

**Read every word on the slide or chart to the audience.** Don't paraphrase. Don't comment as you go along. Read it all.

Some presenters think it is unnecessary, even childish, to read verbatim. But no matter what you do, your audience will read what's in front of their eyes. If you are saying something else, you will distract and confuse them.

Once you've read everything up there, you can comment on it or expand on it. You will no longer be competing with your slides or charts for your audience's attention.

If your style is to ad-lib, put only key words or phrases on your charts or slides.

---

### Problems

1. Price

2. Quality control

3. Japan

4. Sweden

---

**Face the audience.** Work from a script, and read from it so you don't have to turn to the screen.

If you want to indicate individual items on slides, use a pointer.

**Prepare a presentation book the audience can keep.** Tell them at the start that you'll give them copies of all slides and charts in a book after the meeting. This will relieve them from taking notes. You'll get their full attention.

**Be strict about timing.** Plan to finish in *less* than the allotted time. Running long shows a lack of discipline, and abbreviates the person-to-person exchange that could tip the decision your way.

Presenters often sprout wings and fly when confronted with an audience. They expand, tell anecdotes—and hate to sit down. If what you've written is exactly on time in rehearsal, you'll probably run over in performance. If you have twenty minutes, write for fifteen.

**Rehearse—always with props.** Edit—to shorten. Organize—to make sure your message is clear. Revise—to make it sound like you, speaking naturally.

Go through your entire presentation at least twice. Only an amateur worries about overpreparing and losing his edge. The better you know what you're doing, the more spontaneous you'll seem.

## How to write a speech

The agony of getting started. Not the specter of the audience, or the work involved, but *where to begin.*

The answer is not to hunt for a great opening. Nor to ask around for the latest joke.

Put down *anything* that gets you into what you want to talk about, no matter how clumsy it seems. Don't worry about it yet. Get rolling; polish it later.

> Many good speech writers eventually get a good opening by crossing out the first paragraph or two of their drafts. They find the opening line halfway down the first page.

Ted Sorensen, President Kennedy's speech writer, says he starts by making notes while reading and thinking about the subject. The notes include actual lines that might be used in the final speech.

Next, he makes a broad outline, with each heading and subheading numbered or lettered.

Then back to the notes, coding them to the outline—A2, C1, and so forth, cutting them apart and piling them up by section.

Only then does he start to write, in longhand—editing along the way. Finally a draft of the speech is typed.

*NOTE:* Ghost writers can help, but your speech must ultimately reflect *you.* Never deliver a speech drafted by someone else before you have revised it to sound like you.

## Some principles for writing speeches

### 1. No speech was ever too short.

Consider what *you* have so often had to sit through.

> An English parson once gave this sermon: "Saint Paul said, 'The wages of sin is death.' I give you notice: They have not been reduced."
> Having said that, he sat down.

Most good talks take less than twenty minutes. You cannot *bore* people into agreeing with you.

### 2. Form a picture of the speaking situation.

Is it an after-dinner address, a lecture, a seminar? Are you the only speaker or one of several? Whom do you follow on the program? Will the audience be sleepy?

Keep the situation in mind as you write. It will make a difference in what you say as well as in how you say it.

### 3. Start with a point of view.

Think about the subject—*what you want to say.* Kennedy's inaugural address started with this point of view:

> *"We observe today not a victory of party but a celebration of freedom, symbolizing an end as well as a beginning, signifying renewal as well as change . . ."*

Your words need not be so lofty, unless you're being inaugurated as President, but you too should start with a point of view. John D. Rockefeller, Jr., had a point of view about "the things that make life most worth living" and launched a speech with these words:

> *"They are the principles on which my wife and I have tried to bring up our family. They are the principles in which my father believed and by which he governed his life. They are the principles, many of them, which I learned at my mother's knee.*
>
> *"They point the way to usefulness and happiness in life, to courage and peace in death."*

When you have something to say, you can say it, like Rockefeller, with great simplicity. Your listeners will be grateful to you for letting them in on something you feel strongly about.

H. L. Mencken compared two speeches by President Harding. The first was on the simple ideals of the Elks:

> *"It was a topic close to his heart, and he had thought about it at length. . . . The result was an excellent speech— clear, logical, forceful, and with a touch of wild, romantic beauty. . . . But when, at a public meeting in Washington, he essayed to deliver an oration on the subject of Dante Alighieri, he quickly became so obscure and absurd that even the Diplomatic Corps began to snicker."*

Ideas that you believe in make good speeches. It helps to keep a speech file with fodder for your talks.

### 4. Avoid clichés.

It may be "an honor and a privilege" to have been invited to speak, but that is not what people came to hear you say.

Plunge into what you want to say. That's what your audience wants to hear.

### 5. You don't have to tell jokes.

Are you funny? In small groups, do you make people laugh? If not, forget it.

If you do tell a joke or anecdote, don't build up to it ("On the way here tonight . . ."). Tell the joke.

Make sure your jokes are relevant to your point. Make sure they're *funny*—by trying them out ahead of time.

### 6. Write your speech to be spoken.

Don't think of it as an oration. Think of it as a conversation with a friend.

Before the final draft is typed, read it aloud several times and edit it—until it sounds like you talking naturally.

## How to deliver a speech effectively

Think about speeches that have impressed you. The speaker seemed to be *talking* to you, not *reading* to you. You've got to establish *contact* with the audience. And that means looking out at the people, not down at the script.

Some speakers have a bag of tricks that make it easier for them merely to glance at the speech now and then, and spend most of their time looking around the room. Ultimately, however, the only way to do this is to *rehearse*. Rehearse what you have to say over and over until you know it almost by heart.

What sets the memorable speaker apart from the ordinary one is confidence and presence. As somebody's mother-in-law says, "You get right up there and pretend you're just as good as anyone else."

The better you know your speech, the more spontaneous you will sound. And the more *confident*.

It is impossible to be objective about your own speaking ability. Listen to yourself rehearse on a tape recorder. Better yet, take the traumatic step of seeing yourself on videotape. A convincing teacher.

---

Seek opportunities to speak in public. The more you do it, the better you will become. People who advance in their careers learn not to mumble—in writing or in speaking.

It sure is encouraging to have such a terrific turnout for Direct Response Day. If the size of this audience is any indication, the direct response business is booming.

And some new figures we have suggest that it's going to keep on booming, as you're going to see in a little while. But first I thought I ought to tell you something about how we laid our hands on those figures, so you won't doubt their reliability when we go through them. It took us a lot of time and work. And it cost us a lot of money.

As a matter of fact, It cost my company $40,000 to send me here today -- and that doesn't even include my airplane "refreshments," as they're called. $40,000 is what we spent to find out what I should say. That's about $1,500 for every minute I'm up here, so I hope I have your attention.

We used the money to make some phone calls last November. We called up 1,541 people -- half of them women, half of them men, all of them adults. It was a nationally representative sample.

We asked them 113 questions about whether or not direct response advertising affects their lives -- and if it does, how it does.

*Lopping off two paragraphs improved this speech.*

# Chapter 7

# Writing a resume – and getting it read

Nothing else you write can make so big a difference in your life as your application for a job.

You should apply in *writing*. When you telephone for a job, you do it at *your* convenience. *You* choose the moment to call. You have no way of knowing whether your potential employer will be free to talk to you, or in the mood. The odds are against his sitting there waiting for your call.

With a letter, your potential employers pick the times that suit them to consider your application. Your qualifications are more likely to receive their due.

Many job applicants fear that their letters will end up in a wastebasket, unread. True, some will. But an employer who throws out letters of application is hardly the sort to welcome phone calls from strangers.

NOTE: *Resume* can be *resumé* or *résumé*, depending on your dictionary. Since few typewriters have accent keys, *resume* is common usage in business correspondence.

## How to get your resume read

Never send a resume without a covering letter. It takes time to go through a resume. Employers decide from the covering letter whether the resume is worth that time.

*Type* your covering letter to make it look businesslike and easy to read, and follow these rules.

### 1. Address an individual, never a title by itself.

Don't address your envelope ATTENTION PERSONNEL DIRECTOR or MANAGER or HEAD OF ACCOUNTING DEPARTMENT. Raphaelson throws out letters addressed only to "Creative Director" on the ground that if the writer is too lazy to find out his name, he will be too lazy to do a good job.

### 2. Spell all names right.

It's astonishing how often job applicants misspell names, including the names of the firms they want to work for. The message that gets through, right off the bat, is: "This applicant can't be seriously interested in working here; he didn't even take the trouble to find out how to spell our name."

Misspelling a name can lose you an interview.

### 3. Identify the sort of job you're applying for.

State it clearly and at once. Say what led you to apply—a want ad, a recommendation from a friend, whatever.

A letter applying for a job as a research analyst started in this mysterious way:

> Dear Ms. Smith:
>
> It's spring already—a time to think about planting seeds. Some seeds are small, like apple seeds. Others are bigger. Coconuts, for example. But big or little, a seed can grow and flourish if it's planted in proper soil.

79

The applicant would have done better to start like this:

> Dear Ms. Smith:
>
> I understand that you are looking for a research analyst.

Better straight to the point, however trite, than roundabout, however ingenious. Ms. Smith wants to know what the letter is *about;* she doesn't have time to play guessing games with her mail. Don't emulate the fellow who had his tonsils removed through his belly button, just to be different.

**4. Pique the interest of the reader.**

You can do that without missing a beat:

> Dear Ms. Smith:
>
> If you've been looking for an experienced research analyst for three full months, then it's strange that in such a small community we didn't know each other until now.

Many job applicants try to attract favorable attention by buttering up a potential employer:

> Dear Ms. Smith:
>
> I have long admired your firm as one of the most reputable and professional in the country. It is clear that your success cannot be attributed to accident or coincidence.

Flattery may still have its uses in business, but *introducing* yourself as a flatterer won't impress most employers.

Here are a few beginnings of covering letters that go straight to the point in interesting ways:

> Dear Ms. Page:
>
> Do you need an exceptionally *fast* accountant? If so, I may be your man.

Dear Ms. Berry:

The word "creative" in your ad in this evening's *Herald* caught my eye. I have no professional experience whatever, but I was voted "most creative" by my graduating class in both high school and college.

Dear Ms. Kilgour:

Our mutual friend Charles Hartigan has urged me to write to you about your plan to create a publicity department. I would like to help you set it up—and I know how to do it, as you can see from my resume.

## 5. Be specific and factual.

Once you've made clear what job you want, then touch on your chief qualifications. Avoid egotistical abstractions:

Ambition mixed with a striving for excellence is one of my strongest assets.

Ask yourself how you would feel *saying* that to a prospective employer. If it would embarrass you in person, don't put it in writing.

So how do you indicate personal characteristics that may be among your most important qualifications? Be specific and factual; offer evidence in support of any claim of ability; and put the claim as modestly as you can:

You'll see from my resume that I've been studying accounting and tax law at night for two years while working full time as a bookkeeper for R. R. Smith. On weekends from January through April 15, I help my uncle, a tax consultant, with his income-tax business.

I draw your attention to all this as an indication of more than ordinary ambition to become a first-class accountant.

81

Touch on your most important accomplishments in the same matter-of-fact style. Cover your pertinent responsibilities.

Never brag, but don't hesitate to cite authentic evidence of your value.

### 6. Be personal, direct and natural.

You are a human being writing to another human being. Neither of you is an institution. You should be businesslike and courteous, but never stiff and impersonal.

The more your letter sounds like *you,* the more it will stand apart from the letters of your competitors. But don't try to dazzle your reader with your sparkling personality. You wouldn't show off in an interview, so why show off in a letter?

If you make each sentence sound the way you would *say* it, across a desk, there will be plenty of personality in your letter.

### 7. Be brief.

Keep your letter short. Most good covering letters are about half a page. Few run longer than a page.

### 8. Propose a specific next step.

You will be writing to a person or to a box number. In either case, close your letter with a clear and precise statement of how you wish to proceed toward an interview.

Avoid such mumblings as:

> Hoping to hear from you soon.
>
> Thank you for your time and consideration.
>
> I'm looking forward to the opportunity of discussing a position with you.

All such conclusions place the burden of the next step on your busy prospective employer. Why make *him* work in *your* interest? Do the job yourself:

> I'll call your office Wednesday afternoon to see if you'd like me to come in for an interview.

> I'm free for an interview every morning until
> 8:45, and Thursdays after 2:30. I'll call your
> office Wednesday afternoon to find out if you
> would like to get together at any of those times.

At this stage you *should* volunteer to telephone: A phone call
now makes things easy for the person at the other end. If you
don't call him, then he has to go to the trouble of calling or
writing you.

If you are writing to a box number, you *can't* take the next
step. But you can make the next step easy for the person
you're writing to. Enclose a self-addressed postcard for him
to fill out:

> ☐ Please call my secretary for an appointment.
> Her name is:_____
> Phone:_____
> ☐ Sorry, you're not quite right for this job.

Or you could end your letter like this:

> If you'd like me to come in for an interview, you
> can reach me at (999) 438-6688, extension 27,
> from 10 A.M. to 1 P.M., and from 2 to 6:30 P.M.
> on working days. I can arrange to get away for a
> couple of hours any day but Monday; best for me
> would be Thursday morning.

The idea is to make it as simple as you possibly can for your
prospective employer to set up an appointment at a time
that's convenient to you.

### 9. Send different letters to different readers.

You will probably want to send the same resume to all potential employers. But you may not want to approach all of them
exactly the same way in your covering letter; you may feel that
certain of your qualifications would be more important to one
employer than to another.

Take the trouble to modify your covering letter for each of them.

## How to write a resume

A resume summarizes the facts about you, your education, and your experience that are pertinent to the job you want.

The purpose of your resume is to make it as easy as possible for a potential employer to decide whether you might be a candidate for the job at hand. A resume *informs the employer* more than it *sells the applicant.* It doesn't *get* you the job; it reveals whether you and the job may be right for each other.

It follows that your resume should stick to standard, conventional forms. An unconventional resume requires the reader to hunt for information. A prospective employer, confronted with a pile of applications, will not be charmed by those that he has to figure out like a puzzle. They waste his time.

Many considerations go into writing a resume. What to put in? What to leave out? What format to use? What order? What style—telegraphic or full sentences? First person or third person?

Here are some suggestions:

### 1. Keep it short.

Try to get it all on one page.

So often, the less experience the applicant has, the longer the resume. If you have little experience, padding won't help. If you have decades of experience, it is all the more impressive if you stick to the highlights.

Beware of abbreviations. Your prospective employer may not know what they mean. Give full names of companies, trade associations, governmental bodies.

## 2. First things first.

Name, address, phone number at the top.

Next, state your job objective—factually, without embellishment. A prospective employer doesn't care if you want a "challenging position." Sometimes we think we would hire, sight unseen, anybody who *didn't* want a challenging position. *Somebody* has to get out all that nonchallenging work every day.

## 3. List jobs starting with the most recent, working backward.

An employer is more interested in what you have been doing lately than in what you did ten years ago.

> *NOTE: If you gained your most relevant experience some years ago on an earlier job, you can call your reader's attention to it by a bold mark in the margin.*

Include everything that might count—your duties on previous jobs, your accomplishments, your promotions.

Forget for the time being that you're going to boil all this down to one page. Put in everything. Then cut the marginal points, the ones that barely apply. Then shorten the rest, even to the extent of writing in telegraphic style—without verbs, articles or connectives.

## 4. Include published work and membership in associations.

If you have published any articles or books, list the most important ones first.

Membership in trade associations, service to the community, honors—list all these, with the most important ones at the top, the rest in reverse chronological order.

## 5. Cover education—and relevant outside interests.

Include all degrees. Leave out high school (unless you're applying for a first job, or you attended an unusual school). Mention hobbies only if they are pertinent.

85

## What to include—and what to leave out

People put the damnedest things in their resumes. The test of what to include is the same for a resume as it is for anything else you write: Is it relevant? Is it true?

Here is a list of items that commonly appear on resumes, with observations on each:

| Items | Observation |
| --- | --- |
| **Name, address, phone number** | Essential. |
| **Age, sex (if your first name is ambiguous, like Lesley or Tony or Kim)** | The law says you cannot be asked. But employers will find out your sex anyway and will get a fair idea of your age. |
| **Job objective** | Essential. |
| **List of jobs** | Essential. |
| **Dates of previous jobs** | If you leave them out, the reader speculates on what you may be trying to hide. Your age? Were you a beach bum for two years? Maybe none of your jobs lasted more than three months? |
| **Special skills, such as knowledge of a foreign language** | Include if there's a chance that they could be relevant. But don't *exaggerate.* You may have to live up to your claim. |
| **Published articles and books** | Include. |

| | |
|---|---|
| **Honors and prizes** | Include if they are genuinely important in your field. |
| **Education** | Amount of detail depends on how far along you are in your career. If you're a sales manager earning $50,000 a year, nobody cares about your grade average. |
| **Height and weight** | Who cares? It will be assumed that you're presentable. |
| | But again, the rule of relevancy prevails. If you're applying for a job as a saleswoman in an exclusive French dress shop, it might not hurt to mention that you're 5'5" and weigh 102 pounds. |
| **Hobbies and travel** | Only if relevant. |
| **Race, religion, nationality, marital status** | The law says you cannot even be *asked* about any of these. It's up to you to include or omit. |
| **References** | Many job applicants state the obvious in a stuffy phrase: "References furnished upon request." Furnish them right there or don't say anything. |
| **Photograph** | Only beginners seem to include their pictures. |

## Make it look professional

You don't need to go to the expense of printing your resumes. Make sure that your resume is typed *perfectly,* without spelling mistakes or typographical errors. Get top-quality photocopies—crisp and black, without smudges.

## Write a follow-up letter

Follow up important interviews with a short note.

A simple thank-you will do. But if you can find something specific to comment on, so much the better. For instance:

> Dear Ms. Oldham:
>
> After I left your office, I realized that we'd talked for more than an hour. It was stimulating—and made the job seem most attractive.
>
> You talked about your need for someone who truly understands the consumer. I spent three years selling stoves door-to-door plus five years in a research firm. I figure I've spent 5000 hours talking person-to-person with some 3000 consumers in 20 states.
>
> I hope to be able to put this experience to work for you.

Whatever you say, don't gush or grovel. Don't exaggerate your appreciation for the interview or your interest in the job. Here, as in everything you write, candor and sincerity will serve you best.

A follow-up letter certifies your interest and sets you apart from your competitors.

## NEIL K. ROMAN

940 Park Avenue
Boston, Massachusetts  10046
666 563-5236

Coles Tower
Bowdoin College
Brunswick, Maine 04011
207-729-5221

Job Objective:        Newspaper Reporter

BUSINESS EXPERIENCE                                    SUMMERS

The New York Times
    Copyboy                                                1979
    Stringer (school year)                                 1978-80

The Falmouth (Mass.) Enterprise
    Reporter, columnist                                    1978

The Regatta Restaurant (Falmouth, Mass.)
    Dishwasher                                             1978

Great Oaks Camp (Oxford, Maine)
    Tennis director                                        1977
    Tennis counselor                                       1975, 1976

EDUCATION

Bowdoin College
    Major.- Government and Legal Studies, Sociology        A.B., 1980
    Dean's list, Magna Cum Laude

    The Bowdoin Orient
    Chairman, Bowdoin Publishing Co.
    Editor-in-Chief
    News, features, sports editorships

    WBOR
    Assistant news director
    Sportscaster

    Varsity squash, Big Brother, Senior interviewer
    Delta Sigma fraternity

Collegiate School (New York, N.Y.)                     1973-1976
    Varsity baseball, captain (two years)
    Varsity soccer, co-captain

Birth date: June 6, 1958
Marital status: Single

Interests: All sports, fishing, reading, politics, movies, rock music

*This resume helped win a first job.*

# Chapter 8

---

# Make it look easy to read

---

Neatness counts.
If what you've written looks formidable or messy or sloppy, your reader braces for an ordeal before reading a word. "This looks like heavy going" is the message you deliver, at first glance.

If what you've written looks easy to take in and get through, you're off to a good start.

Here are some ways to make everything you write look *professional*—inviting to read, easy to understand and simple to refer to.

**1. Start with a heading.**

Put it top center in capital letters. This orients your reader at once.

OFFICE CLOSES FRIDAY NOON

PURSE THIEF AT LARGE

**2. Keep paragraphs short.**

Wherever you see a long paragraph, break it into two or more short ones.

90

**3. Use typographic devices for clarity and emphasis.**

For extra emphasis, underline entire sentences. When under-lining sentences or phrases, <u>use a single continuous underline</u> rather than a <u>choppy-looking</u> <u>underline</u>, <u>one</u> <u>word</u> <u>at</u> <u>a</u> <u>time</u>, which slows reading.

> To stress key ideas, put them into indented paragraphs. This emphasizes them by set-ting them apart.

Number your points. Numbered or lettered points look best when the numbers or letters are typed a couple of spaces to the left of the text margin, like the *a.* and *b.* that follow.

> a. Typewriters can't produce printer's effects, such as the boldface we use for numbers in this chapter, to carry the eye from point to point.
>
> b. "Hanging" your letters and numbers in the margin makes your divisions and subdivi-sions easier to follow.

Another way to call attention to a key point is with a hand-written mark in the margin. Doing it in color is even better.

**4. Use upper and lower case.**

Never use all capitals except for headings. They are hard to read when they run on for more than a few words.

**5. Break up large masses of type.**

Use subheads. Write them to pull the reader into the next paragraph, as above.

Type them in upper and lower case, underline them, and leave plenty of space above and below.

### 6. Use space to separate paragraphs.

It looks neater than indents, in typewritten material.

Use single spacing between lines, double spacing between paragraphs. Drafts of documents for which you are soliciting comments should be triple-spaced throughout. It makes editing easier.

### 7. Handle numbers consistently.

Newspapers generally spell out numbers for ten and under, use numerals for 11 and up.

It is easier to grasp big numbers when you write $60 million rather than $60,000,000.

### 8. Make charts easy to handle—and interesting.

If your document includes wide charts, don't make the reader turn it sideways to read them. Use horizontal foldouts.

Consider whether your charts need to be in the body of your document at all. Might they go at the end, as appendices? Your document will look less formidable if it is uninterrupted by graphs and charts.

Put them in color, if possible, particularly if they have to go in the body rather than in an appendix. Color adds vitality and variety.

Number your appendices and separate them clearly with tabs. This makes them easy to find.

### 9. Make it perfect.

No typos, no strikeovers, no misspellings, no smudges. Nothing to distract the reader. Nothing to offend the eye.

Never use a worn-out typewriter ribbon. Crisp black type looks smart and important, and is inviting to read.

Photocopy equipment should be adjusted to reproduce the sharpness of your original without smudges or dirty border marks. Poor photocopies look cheap and ugly, and discourage reading.

**10. Number your pages, even in early drafts.**

If inserted material messes up the order, use 1A, 1B, and so on. Nothing is more annoying than trying to refer to an item in an unnumbered paper.

---

Before you hand over your final draft for typing, run your eye over it with these techniques in mind:

What can you do to make it look more interesting? Where will your meaning be illuminated by subheadings, indents, underlines, enumeration?

Write for the eye as well as the mind.

# Ogilvy & Mather
*Advertising*

2 EAST 48 STREET, NEW YORK 10017 (212) 688-6100

*From:* David Ogilvy  *Date* December 10, 1979  *Memorandum*

*To:* Board of Directors

Last week I gave a talk to the Forum Club in Houston. I opened
with something you may find useful: "Opinion Research Corporation
recently put this question to a sample of the general public:'How
much after-tax profit do you think the average manufacturer makes
on the products they sell?' The answer was 32 percent. The public is under the impression that manufacturers make a profit of
32 percent. For oil companies, they said 57 percent. The public
thinks this is excessive. I don't blame them.

"They were then asked, 'What do you consider would be a reasonable
profit?' The answer was 26 percent. In other words, if manufacturers made a profit of 26 percent, the general public would think
that was reasonable. What would the Great American Public think
if they knew how much profit manufacturers really make? It's not
26 percent, but five percent. If the public knew this, they would
be utterly amazed.

"The politicians know the facts. They know what profit levels
really are. But they also know that the public doesn't know. Hence
their cynical, demagogic attacks on profits. If you believe as I
do, that profits are the life blood of our economic system, don't
you think it is time to tell the public that profits are not 32
percent, as they believe, but a beggarly five percent?"

D.O.

*Hard to read.*

# Ogilvy & Mather
*Advertising*

2 EAST 48 STREET, NEW YORK 10017 (212) 688-6100

*From:* David Ogilvy  *Date* December 10, 1979  *Memorandum*

*To:* Board of Directors

## PUBLIC OPINION AND PROFITS

Last week I gave a talk to the Forum Club in Houston. I opened with something you may find useful:

"Opinion Research Corporation recently put this question to a sample of the general public:

'How much after-tax profit do you think the average manufacturer makes on the products they sell?'

The answer was 32 percent. The public is under the impression that manufacturers make a profit of 32 percent.

For oil companies, they said 57 percent. The public thinks this is excessive. I don't blame them.

They were then asked, 'What do you consider would be a reasonable profit?' The answer was 26 percent. In other words, if manufacturers made a profit of 26 percent, the general public would think that was reasonable.

What would the Great American Public think if they knew how much profits manufacturers really make?

It's not 26 percent, but five percent. If the public knew this, they would be utterly amazed.

The politicians know the facts. They know what profit levels really are. But they also know that the public really doesn't know. Hence their cynical, demagogic attacks on profits.

If you believe as I do, that profits are the life blood of our economic system, don't you think it is time to tell the public that profits are not 34 percent, as they believe, but a beggarly five percent?"

D.O.

*Easy to read.*

# Chapter 9

# Edit everything you write

Never send out the first draft of anything important. The better the writer, the less satisfied he is likely to be with his first draft, or even with his second. Good writers consider editing *an essential part of the writing process,* not just a final polishing up. Edit your work:

- to shorten
- to sharpen and clarify
- to simplify
- to check for accuracy and precision
- to improve order and logic
- to make sure nothing is left out
- to review tone
- to examine everything from the reader's point of view.

The first rule: If it isn't essential, *cut it out.* Go through your draft once asking only this question: *What can I get rid of?* Cut unnecessary words, phrases, sentences, paragraphs.

> *Mark Twain said that writers should strike out every third word on principle: "You have no idea what vigor it adds to style."*

Go through your draft a second time with these questions in mind:

### 1. Are you mumbling?

In putting together a first draft, it speeds things up to get *something* on paper, even if it only approximates what you want to say. But never settle for an approximation in your final draft.

Have you chosen the verbs and adjectives that express your meaning precisely? Could you be less abstract and more down-to-earth? Scrutinize every important word.

### 2. Have you got things in the best order?

This point was originally number six instead of number two. In editing, we decided it was *second* in importance—and closely related to point three.

Good writers shift things around a lot. They often use scissors and Scotch tape to reassemble entire sections.

### 3. Are there any holes in your argument?

Put yourself in your reader's shoes. Does everything follow logically?

Don't expect your reader to leap from point to point like a goat on a rocky hillside. Make sure your trail is clear, smooth and well marked.

### 4. Are your facts right?

Check all statistics and statements of fact. A single bad error can undermine your reader's confidence in your paper.

In particular, check quotations. "I quote a lot," says David Ogilvy, the advertising man. "I always check, even when I am in no doubt. And I am *always* wrong."

## 5. Is the tone right?

Too stiff? Too chummy? Lacking in sympathy? Rude? Again put yourself in your reader's place and change anything that you, as a reader, might find offensive.

## An example of editing

Here are five instances, taken from a single paper, of how editing shortened, sharpened and clarified what the writer was trying to say:

| First draft | Second draft |
| --- | --- |
| Consumer perception of the brand changed very positively. | Consumer rating of the brand soared. |
| Generate promotion interest through high levels of advertising spending. | Advertise heavily to build interest in promotions. |
| Move from product advertising to an educational campaign, one that would instruct viewers on such things as . . . | Move from product advertising to an educational campaign on subjects like . . . |
| Using the resources of our organization in Europe, in addition to our Chicago office, we have been able to provide management with alternatives they had previously been unaware of. | Our offices in Europe and Chicago produced alternatives that management hadn't known about. |

| | |
|---|---|
| Based on their small budget, we have developed a media plan which is based on efficiency in reaching the target audience. | We developed a media plan that increases the efficiency of their small budget by focusing on prospects. |

## Two secrets of editing

You will multiply the effectiveness of your editing if you *let time elapse between drafts.*

And if you *solicit the advice of other people.*

Have your draft typed clean. Set it aside. Get away from it at least overnight. Then come back to it in the morning.

You'll see it with new eyes. Imperfections that were invisible the day before will now pop out at you. Through some alchemy of time, you'll know what to do about them.

When you ask for comments from other people—colleagues, friends, anybody whose opinion you respect—you're putting them to work for you. If somebody's suggestions are helpful, say "Thank you" and use them. If you disagree with them, say "Thank you" and *don't* use them.

No need to argue or prove your consultant wrong. It's your work and you are making the decisions.

You'll find that nearly everybody will spot something you overlooked. It can be invaluable just to discover that a point isn't clear.

David Ogilvy sends drafts of all important papers to several of his associates with the handwritten injunction, "Please improve." He has been the beneficiary of so many improvements that he now lives in a 60-room castle in France.

~~Respect~~ *Plunge* that honor and exercise ~~that privilege by~~ plunging ~~at once~~ into what you want to say. That's what your audience wants to ~~listen to.~~ *hear.*

5. You don't have to tell jokes ~~or anecdotes.~~

   Are you funny? In small groups, do you make people laugh? If not, forget it.

   If you do tell a joke *(an anecdote,)* don't build up to it ("On the way here tonight..."). ~~Plunge into the joke.~~ *Tell the joke.*

   ~~Test your jokes or anecdotes in advance. And~~ Make sure *your jokes* ~~they~~ are relevant to ~~the~~ *your* point. ~~you are making~~ *Make sure they're funny — by trying them out ahead of time.*

6. Write ~~it~~ *your speech* to be spoken.

   Don't think of it as an oration. Think of ~~what you are~~ *it* ~~writing~~ as a conversation with ~~someone.~~ *a friend.*

   Before the final draft is typed, read it aloud several times and edit it ~~along the way~~ -- until it sounds like you talking naturally.

   How To Deliver A Speech Effectively

   Now that you've written a terrific speech a book on writing should drop the subject and move on. But you can't. You've got to deliver the thing.

*Editing improved even the fourth draft of this book.*

# Chapter 10

# Finding the time to write well

Writing better does not mean writing *more*. There is paper enough in our lives now, and precious little time to read it.

This book has suggested some of the ways that improving your writing can save time for other people. But what about *your* time?

While you respect the time of others, you must also protect your own.

It takes time to write well. Business authority Peter Drucker cautions us against assuming there are 24 hours in a day—or even eight hours. He estimates that in a typical workday there are perhaps one or two hours that you can use productively. The difference between *busy* executives and *effective* ones is how they use time.

Look for time-savers to help you cope with the paper you receive and respond to in writing. The level of paper rises as you do. It takes skill to dispatch it.

Try to handle paper only once. Decide quickly whether to answer it, file it or toss it in the wastebasket. The biggest time waster is shuffling things from one pile to another while you drown in a sea of indecision.

Answer easy items instantly. Write your comments directly on letters and memos, and return them *at once.* Or send short handwritten notes of direction, praise or criticism.

Save dictation for more formal responses, but brief ones only. Longer answers require more organization and less verbosity than most people can achieve while dictating.

There is no rule that says you must answer (or file) everything that is sent to you. If in doubt, toss it out.

Some papers require study. Read them actively. Get to the principal arguments, and decide what must be done.

> *Consider a "maturing file" for knotty problems. Many disappear if given time. Others call for more thought.*

All this will help you clear the decks—at the office or at home—for the more important parts of your job. High among them will be the major papers you write.

Indeed, writing important papers may be the most important of all your functions. Well-written documents clarify issues, cut off fruitless squabbles, provide clear direction, and get things done.

It is up to you to decide when, where and what to write, and *to make the time to write well.*

# Afterword

## Other books that will help you write better

Most people who write well read a lot. They read many kinds of good writing—good fiction, good history, good journalism.

If you want to write better, read E. B. White. Read Hemingway. Read *The New Yorker.* Read the *Economist.* Read William James and Mark Twain and H. L. Mencken, Rebecca West and Barbara Tuchman and Art Buchwald.

You'll get the shapes and rhythms of good writing into your head. Reading good writing will help you more than reading *about* good writing—and it is a lot more fun.

But there *are* books on writing, and some reference books, that you may find helpful. Among the best:

**The Elements of Style,** *William Strunk, Jr., and E. B. White, Macmillan (81 pages).* No other book has helped so many writers, professional and nonprofessional, to steer away from vulgarism and to find their own modes of expression. Concise, comprehensive and elegant.

**The Golden Book of Writing,** *David Lambuth and others, Penguin (79 pages).* "The best brief handbook on writing," says *The New York Times.* Useful tips for business executives or students.

**Plain Letters,** *a Records Management Handbook published by the federal government and available from the Superintendent of Documents, Washington, D.C. 20402 (51 pages).* An excellent manual by an anonymous government author. Contains a "watchlist" of overworked and misused words—and a useful set of questions to ask about any letter or memorandum.

**Webster's New Collegiate Dictionary,** *G. & C. Merriam Co.* One of the few reference works that draws distinctions between many near-synonyms, clearly explaining subtle differences of meaning.

**American Heritage Dictionary,** *Houghton-Mifflin.* A unique "usage panel" reports on what constitutes good contemporary usage of hundreds of words and expressions. (Also draws distinction between near-synonyms.)

**On Writing Well,** *William Zinsser, Harper & Row (176 pages).* More for the professional writer of nonfiction than for the business writer. But enlightening, entertaining and wise—well worth reading if you get hooked on improving your writing.

**Successful Direct Marketing Methods,** *Bob Stone, Crain Books (334 pages).* In the opinion of many professionals, this is the most complete and authoritative book on direct marketing. It covers every aspect of selling through the mails.

**Strictly Speaking,** *Edwin Newman, The Bobbs-Merrill Co. (224 pages).* The best attack on jargon, clichés and errors.

**Language in Thought and Action,** *S. I. Hayakawa, Harcourt Brace Jovanovich, Inc. (307 pages).* The basic book on semantics, a study of the relationship between language and behavior. A stimulating guide to accurate thinking, reading, listening and writing.

**Make the Most of Your Best,** *Dorothy Sarnoff, Doubleday (228 pages).* Invaluable advice from an authority on public speaking. Covers everything from small presentations to major speeches, from preparing a lecture script to overcoming nerves.

**Watch Your Language,** *Theodore M. Bernstein, Atheneum (276 pages).* The former assistant managing editor of *The New York Times* has put together, in dictionary form, his commonsense thoughts on hundreds of questions on writing that come up regularly. Authoritative but in no way pedagogical.

**The Bible.** Still the best demonstration of the power of simple writing.

# About the Authors

Kenneth Roman and Joel Raphaelson are senior officers of Ogilvy & Mather, a major advertising agency noted for its interest in good writing.

Kenneth Roman is President of the company and co-author of *How to Advertise*, which has become a standard text in the business and has been published in six other countries. Joel Raphaelson is Creative Head of the agency's Chicago office and a frequent lecturer on writing and other subjects.

| DATE DUE | | |
|---|---|---|
| | | |
| | | |
| | | |
| | | |
| | | |
| | | |
| | | |
| | | |
| | | |
| | | |